Channeling

Channeling

WHAT IT IS *and*
HOW TO DO IT

LITA DE ALBERDI

SAMUEL WEISER, INC.

York Beach, Maine

*This book is dedicated to my dearest husband Marco
and my beloved son Luke*

*Without the assistance of the guides, the angels, the Masters and
Beings of Light and my beloved family, this book could never have
been written. They have inspired me, they have tirelessly brought
ideas and material to me, and they have supported me throughout
this project.*

First published in 2000 by
Samuel Weiser, Inc.
P. O. Box 612
York Beach, ME 03910-0612
www.weiserbooks.com

08 07 06 05 04 03 02 01 00
10 9 8 7 6 5 4 3 2 1

Library of Congress Cataloging-in-Publication Data

de Alberdi, Lita.
    Channeling: what it is and how to do it / Lita de Alberdi.
        p. cm.
    Includes bibliographical references (p.) and index.
    ISBN 1-57863-145-9 (paper : alk. paper)
    1. Channeling (Spiritualism) I. Title.
BF1286 .D43 2000
133.9'1—dc21   99-049279

Cover design by Kathryn Sky-Peck

Printed in the United States of America
BJ

The paper used in this publication meets the minimum requirements of the American
National Standard for Information Sciences—Permanence of Paper for Printed
Library Materials Z39.48-1992 (R1997).

CONTENTS

ACKNOWLEDGEMENTS

I would like to thank the following for their invaluable help: my husband Marco for all his support and love; my mother, Rhoda Gray, for her love and her unfailing belief in me; my son Luke for his loving humour; Kate and Wayne Benson, loyal friends and brother and sister on the path; Ian Adamson, brother and dearest companion on the path; Llee Heflin for sparking me into action; Lynda Hannam, Pam Osborne, Jackie Reeve, Jen Altman, Tina Northcott, Jan Matthews, Janie Stubbs, Carole Wildor, Gill Holland, Gaynor Perkins, Sarah Hurst, Jane Reid, Jennie Gray, Katie Le May, Audrey Lowery and all the many, many students whose support and love mean so much to me; Caroline Root, the world's best acupuncturist, who keeps me healthy; Sanaya Roman and Duane Packer for their wise teachings, support and help in my path of spiritual growth; Lindsay Senecal for her teaching, her love and her wisdom; Karen Knowler for her wonderful help and great ideas; Piatkus for publishing this book; and, last but not least, my wonderful guides Ortan and Shalaya.

Deep peace of the running wave to you.
Deep peace of the flowing air to you.
Deep peace of the quiet earth to you.
Deep peace of the gentle night to you.
Moon and stars pour their healing light on you.
Deep peace of the Light of the World to you.
                              A GAELIC BLESSING

INTRODUCTION

My journey into the Light began from my very first memories of life. An only child, I spent a great deal of time on my own and was blessed with a clear awareness of the existence of other beings and other dimensions beyond the everyday reality inhabited by those around me.

When I was very small I knew instinctively how to call upon the angels to keep me safe during the night. Like many children I was afraid of the dark, but when I called upon them I knew I would be protected. I used to lie in bed with the covers firmly over my head. Eventually I would summon up the courage to peep out into the dark, by which time, of course, my eyes were dark-adjusted. The curtains in my room had a pattern that always resolved into faces if I focused on it. This used to terrify me, and I would have to go back under the covers for a considerable time before I could recover my courage and peep out again.

Before I could call upon the angels I believed that I had to have enough courage to see them arrive and take up their positions, so only when I had my nerve up would I peep out and in my mind ask God to send them. Almost instantly four seemingly massive winged angels would materialize, one at each corner of my small bed. They would stand strong and firm, with the faces of young men or women – they seemed sexless to me then, although I never really thought about the matter.

For many years, all through my childhood and beyond, I used to invoke the angels in this way. Because I went to a Christian school I always thought that everyone could see angels – it never occurred to me that they didn't. Angels seemed to be an important part of the Christian Churches' teachings. Commonly spoken of, they were the messengers of God – as in the angel who came to Mary to tell her about the birth of Jesus. So it seemed very natural that angels would be there to take care of me.

I firmly believe that many other people can remember that kind of awareness as well; unfortunately, as we grow up we are trained to forget it. My father was a sceptic and had no personal belief in God or anything other than the material world. My mother had psychic abilities, but she had never been trained and so, for her, much of what she experienced generated fear. But such fear soon dissolves as one comes to understand that sensing and seeing subtle energies is completely natural for us. In my own work, training channels, I see students experience great joy and express tremendous enthusiasm as they find themselves able to harness this potential.

During my childhood I had many deep experiences of God and higher states of consciousness. I was confirmed into the Anglican Church and took Communion, but in my teens I was disappointed to find that the Church could not answer my questions about the universe, about God and the reasons for our existence here on earth. It could not even come up with a convincing answer about life before or after our present existence.

I began to read everything I could about different religions, such as Buddhism and Hinduism, and about the occult. At that time there was no New Age literature, but I did get a very thorough grounding in religion, theosophy, magic, the Kabbalah and lots more. It became clear to me that there was a lot more to human existence than I had been led to believe by conventional wisdom, but at that time there were very few 'alternative' approaches that were widely known. I was strongly influenced by the work of the Russian teacher Gurdjieff and his follower Ouspensky; their theories about humankind being 'asleep' explained a lot to me. My own experience was that people seemed to be on 'automatic' – not questioning, not thinking about their existence and the reason for it. I used a number of Gurdjieff's practices to help me awaken and stay awake as a conscious being. I found a lot of inspiration also in the Kabbalistic writings of Israel Regardie, especially his detailed descriptions of practices such as the Middle Pillar exercise as explained in his book *The Art of True Healing*, which I thoroughly recommend. This exercise involves toning and breathing techniques to steady and centre your energy, connecting you with the light and energy of the higher realms. Alice Bailey, a channel through whom her 'guide', a Tibetan Buddhist master known as Djwhal Khul, made his ideas known, was a further influence: she both fascinated and confused me.

In my late teens I met my first spiritual teacher/mentor. At last here was someone as strange as me! He seemed to speak my language, and had read even more than I had. Gently he guided me through the many paths to knowledge, stressing the importance of individual practice: it was not enough just to read books – you had to *do* something as well. I began to meditate regularly and to follow various spiritual practices.

In my early twenties I travelled to America where I met an astrologer who lived in a Native American teepee in the mountains of Vermont. After reading my astrological chart he confirmed that I would be following the path of growth – my own higher purpose – in this life. It was a turning point for my growth because he recognized that service would be the key to my life. I also joined a Gurdjieffian group and continued my practice in this tradition. During this time I came to understand much more about individual freedom, realizing that my path was just as valid as anyone else's. I developed a deep interest in psychology and trained as a counsellor, working as a volunteer on a Hotline (like the Samaritans in England) and wrestling with my own psyche, especially problems like the negative ego (the part of us that generates fear, anger, jealously, lack of self-esteem and so on).

On my return to England I studied psychology and sociology for several years, making this study part of my path of spiritual growth. Regardie says that to pursue an interest in the esoteric disciplines it is essential to know yourself. I agree with him: with self-knowledge and understanding everything else will follow. You don't need to study psychology as such, but you do need to understand your own strengths and weaknesses, the little traps of the negative ego.

A few years later I found I was able to hold and maintain a conscious connection with the higher realms where the guides, like Alice Bailey's Tibetan master, are. But at that time the concept of channelling was virtually unknown and, whilst I understood that the information I was receiving was from a higher source, I didn't identify my guide as a 'personality' for some time afterwards and I certainly didn't call it channelling. I simply found that I could open up to this higher information. I remember saying to my partner then, 'Just ask me anything and I will know the answer.' My explanation was that I was connecting to the Karmic Records, that dimension where all that has been known and all that will be known is available, and which is sometimes known as the Universal Mind.

Later I began to channel a guide called Iskera, using the techniques developed by Sanaya Roman and Duane Packer through their guides Orin and DaBen. Ortan took over as my guide on the death of my teacher. Iskera explained that our work together was done. Ortan explained that it was now my time to begin to teach, that he was a teacher guide and that this would be our work together.

At this point I realized that I had to give up my 'normal' life and commit myself fully to my spiritual path. This was when I began teaching classes on meditation, spiritual growth and development, and giving individual readings with Ortan. Since then my focus has been on giving classes called Awakening Your Light Body (and classes for those who already have awakened light bodies), Opening to Channel, Working with Your Guide, and Advanced Channelling. Healing classes are also an important part of my work.

I have found the light body work, as developed by Orin and DaBen, profoundly transformative. Much of the work I have channelled and now teach, such as ascension, is for light body graduates. The awakening of the light body seems to be a major and fundamental step at this time of change (see Chapter 2).

This book is a result of my experience as a channel and a teacher of channelling. So many of my students have asked for a book, and my guide Ortan has pushed me from his side too! The book explains what channelling is and how you too can connect with your own guide. For those who want to develop their channelling, various chapters deal with particular kinds of work such as reading auras, reading chakras and reading on past lives.

We all have a guide. Reading this book will help you to understand that you will experience no difficulty in connecting with your own guide, sharing this marvellous experience and opening yourself to spiritual growth.

1

ALL ABOUT CHANNELLING AND GUIDES

I am dwelling in a form which to you would appear perhaps as simply a shimmer, as a movement within the air.

ORTAN

WHAT IS CHANNELLING?

Channelling is the means by which you can make a direct connection with a non-physical or discarnate being called a guide (see p.10). It is a process of consciously connecting with entities who exist on other planes of reality, and those who do so are known as channels. Throughout the history of humanity people have channelled various types of entities.

I prefer to distinguish channelling from the work of mediums. Mediums work with dead people – entities that have been in existence as human beings and have now passed on. The focus for mediums is to prove the existence of life after death, but the focus for channels is less narrow. The work of mediums is, however, extremely valuable, as it is important to realize that there is an existence after death, and their work is complementary to that of channels.

Channelling involves deliberately shifting your awareness to achieve an expanded state of consciousness. You have to learn to concentrate and to get your own thoughts out of the way so that you can become receptive to your higher guidance.

The ancient Egyptians, for example, channelled the 'God' energy, while in ancient Greece the Delphic Oracle was frequently consulted. Even in the Bible, Old Testament prophets channelled energies which they identified as 'God'. Madame Blavatsky, the founder of theosophy, channelled a series of masters and as a result wrote *Isis Unveiled,* a classic work about ancient religions and their revival. Alice Bailey, inspired by her Tibetan master, set up the Arcane School.

Probably one of the best-known recent channels is Edgar Cayce, who would sink into a state of hypnosis in which he would provide astonishingly accurate readings for his clients. Jane Roberts and her guide Seth brought through huge amounts of information in their books. Finally, Sanaya Roman is a gifted channel who has helped thousands on to their path of growth and personal development. Some of Sanaya's books are listed in the bibliography on p.159.

Some people hear clear words from their guides; others see pictures which they describe; and still others just get a sense of what the guide is trying to convey. As you do more and more channelling the guides help to develop this gift of connecting.

Guides exist outside of space and time, and as a result they are able to be with you at any time you wish. They do not have physical bodies, although they may well once have done on either this or another planet. However, such guides were frequently teachers even when they were physical and since their passing over they have continued to develop spiritually.

A gateway into love

The higher realms where the guides exist are full of love (see Chapter 2 for a discussion of levels and dimensions). Your guide's aim is to make you more powerful, more independent and more confident. Your guide is full of love, compassion and understanding for you. Your guide knows that you have a higher purpose, which represents the real heart of your reason for choosing to be born at this time and in these circumstances. I believe that, before birth, each of us is encoded by our soul with a 'mission' – our higher purpose for this lifetime. We consciously choose this with our soul's guidance.

A clearer viewpoint

When you channel it is like climbing to the top of a mountain. You will discover more about yourself and others and see your life from a higher, broader perspective, which helps you to discover the deeper meaning of situations in which you find yourself.

A means of self-help

As a channel you can learn to do things effortlessly if you choose. But you will still struggle if you choose that. This does not mean that everything will come to you, and that you can just relax and do nothing. What it does mean is that you can gain a greater sense of what you want to create and will be able to find easier ways to bring it about. Channelling won't solve all your problems – it will only change you in the ways you want to change. You are the one who takes action and you are still responsible for your own life, but working with a high-level guide does accelerate your growth opportunities and your learning curve. Channelling a guide will help you to see yourself and others with greater compassion and objectivity and less judgement.

The purpose of channelling

When you decide to open to channelling your guide, what you are doing is bringing the guide's energy down to the physical plane which you inhabit. Guides have no physical form, but you do – you are the receiver of their energy and you are the transformer of their energy. You transform their energy impulses into words that can be understood by other people, or you may transform the energy into music or painting, or you may choose to channel healing frequencies for the assistance of others.

Spiritual work is about bringing the frequencies of spiritual realms into our everyday reality, grounding those frequencies so that they can be perceived by other people. Channelling is just a form of that – grounding in the energy of your guide and the things that your guide wants to share with you, and through you with other people.

In short, when you learn to channel you are creating many opportunities for personal growth and development, as well as for service to humanity. Channelling will obviously result in different changes for different people, but typically people who channel become more self-confident, happier, clearer about their path and their choices, less selfish, less stressed over life's problems, calmer, more loving and psychologically much stronger. One of my students told me that she and her guide have developed a marvellous way of bringing healing for her physical body: she channels this energy into her body and within minutes she can begin to shake off health problems such as colds and viruses.

How can you tell if you are ready to channel?

Good channels are those who enjoy thinking for themselves. They are often on a path of service to others, such as healing; they are also independent, open-minded, self-confident, sensitive and in touch with their feelings. They are people who enjoy learning and who are open to new skills, ideas and knowledge. The qualities that guides seem to value are dedication, enthusiasm and the willingness to be a channel. You need to have a willingness to make your life work at every level, and to attract a high-level guide it helps if you have spiritual interests, a desire to help others and a concern for their wellbeing. Channelling always seems to help others in some way.

A common fear amongst people who want to channel is that they will be the one who can't do it. They are very concerned that they aren't ready, they aren't worthy and so on. So how *do* you know that you are ready to channel? Everyone who completes the channelling courses we teach does actually channel during the class. They may not be destined to be verbal channels, but they all make a good, strong connection with their guide so that after the class they can develop the relationship to support them. I firmly believe that people are only drawn to the courses we teach when they are ready to use the material. Ultimately only you can know if you are ready to channel. But even when you are ready, you may still feel very anxious about whether you really can do it. This anxiety is really just a reflection of the excitement you are feeling deep down at the possibility that you can be a genuine channel. Fear is merely one end of a continuum, and excitement the other.

Other fears about channelling

At the School of the Living Light we have taught many people to channel and there are some fears that come up frequently. One is that channelling will turn you into a space cadet, out of touch with reality. In fact it seems to have the opposite effect – people often report that they feel more grounded, centred and better able to deal effectively with their daily lives. Your guide can be of great assistance at a day-to-day level.

Another fear is that you will be taken over, as I mentioned earlier. But channelling does not entail a surrender of control. One respondent in our recent research with channels said of her guide, 'Light Angel is always close but does not intrude in my life unless I ask for help and assistance. Light Angel does not make decisions for me but helps me look at things in an even and fair way.' You are likely to find that your sense of self is greatly enhanced, as if contact with the Other creates a greater awareness of your own identity. You may find that it becomes easier to set limits and to define your personal boundaries.

Yet another fear is that you will become vulnerable to lower entities. Actually you can recognize these lower entities by their negativity. Once you have a good connection with a high-level guide, this guide will protect you whether or not you are channelling.

WHAT ARE GUIDES?

I have already mentioned guides in various contexts, but a clear explanation will be helpful at this stage. In brief, guides are beings who have chosen to work with us at this time to enable us to access high-level information to assist in our growth. Guides connect with us at a high level called the soul level. The information they bring is then transmitted into our physical brain as pulses of energy.

Encouragement rather than control

High-level guides encourage you to rely on your inner guidance even over their guidance; they never try to take over or to control you. In fact the situation is quite the opposite: guides encourage you to grow and support you in what you choose to do. Ortan always reminds me that it is a law of the universe that you have to ask. What he means by this is that *you* have to choose to ask for help in whatever it is you are doing.

Guides have far too much respect for us to intervene without being asked. They see that we must learn the lessons that our soul chose for us in this lifetime; if we want to do this alone, so be it. But you don't have to do it alone ever again when you have chosen to channel your guide. All you need to do is ask for help. The guides will do all they can from their side to offer the highest lessons and the highest experiences you can have.

Connecting with your guide

Often guides begin to connect with you in your dreams. A very common experience is waking in the night and not knowing why. Ortan explains that the veils between the realms are very thin at night, especially between about three and four in the morning, so this is the time when people have vivid dreams of guides or are awoken by their guide trying to contact them. You may find that you are becoming interested in channelling, going for readings, attending talks on channelling, meeting channels or reading books on the subject. You may be very interested in your spiritual path and keen to know more about your work and higher purpose in this lifetime. You may feel you are looking for something but are unsure of what it will be, or you may feel ready to have a more open connection to the higher realms.

If you do ask for a guide to assist you, one will begin to work with you. In your meditations ask for a guide to begin working with you. Sometimes during meditation you get guidance that seems to be of a higher wisdom than your own. As your connection with your guide strengthens and deepens you may think more often about channelling a guide, and although you may have doubts and questions about channelling you will feel that you want to know more.

Different types of guide

Although people talk of guides in general there are different types and each has a different purpose. The guide aligns with the purpose of the person who is doing the channelling. In this chapter I would like to share with you material that my guide

Ortan has asked be included, specifically about myself as a channel, the types of guides and the names of guides.

This book was written because Ortan started to bring through information about a book on channelling. On 10 August 1995 he suggested that: *'The book could discuss the guides, their nature, the types of guides, the types of people perhaps who connect in to channel and what happens afterwards of course. This is of interest and also to tell people how these guides, we guides will assist them in the changes to come, to tell them that there is nothing to fear in these changes.'* Ortan also envisaged the book being accompanied by meditation tapes. We have since made these with his assistance, and information on how to obtain them can be found on p.158.

Ortan wants humanity to understand that there are major changes going on at this time, changes that are resulting in a huge surge of interest in channelling, in meditation, in spiritual development generally. Ortan is very keen for us to know that there is nothing to fear, that although the changes may be great we will be safe and protected. The key to an easy transition in this time is to dedicate yourself to realizing your own potential as a spiritual being who has chosen to take a human body at this time. It is of fundamental importance that all of us who are now awakening focus on understanding ourselves as spiritual beings, and that we start to open more and more to higher guidance and higher wisdom through channelling.

Guides to help our awakening

Many souls are now awakening and remembering. These souls need help to reach the path of light and initiation, and this is where the guides and channels come in. They are here to help us in the very important process of transformation into beings who know what they are and why they are here. I believe that this awakening process is cumulative: as more and more people awaken to higher realities, they make it easier for others to follow.

My own experience with guides has been that they are always available, very loving, and often have a deep sense of compassion and service to humanity. Some have had earth lives and others have not. In a sense this is of no importance: those who did have earth lives have long since evolved beyond the need to keep incarnating. See p.124 for Ortan's words on the effects of channelling.

Guides can be experienced, as I have mentioned, in a whole range of ways. Some people see their guides: they have a strong visual sense of the guide as a being. Often these seem to be the guides who did incarnate, and the form that is perceived by the channel is a reflection of that last incarnation. For example, there seems to be a considerable number of Native American guides working with humanity at present. I have channelled for people with such guides and had very strong visual impressions of their energy and that of their animals – many of them work directly with animal energies. In the Native American tradition, many teachers worked directly with animal spirits. Indeed, sometimes the initiate seemed actually to 'become' the animal.

Other guides are just felt as they join their channel. It may be a sensation as subtle as a deepening of their breathing, a gentle tingling around the top of the head, a shift in posture or an emotional response like intense happiness or deep love.

My own guides explain

I have two guides working with me at present. Ortan, who has worked with me since the death of my great friend and spiritual teacher, and Shalaya who joined me later in 1994. Both have given me information about themselves which may help you to understand how guides themselves view guides.

Ortan explains that he has no physical form at all, and cannot be seen or heard with the normal sensing mechanisms of ears or eyes: '*I am dwelling in a form which to you would appear perhaps as simply a shimmer, as a movement within the air.*' He goes on to explain that in his dimension, which he describes as a place of light, all are in service to the divine. The beings there have some sort of a community, working together and communicating with each other – they are all connected energetically to make one consciousness. Many of these beings have evolved from incarnations on the earth and other planets. In this dimension some of the entities have pledged to assist humanity in awakening to their spiritual potential and in starting on a path of growth. He stresses that in his dimension there is a constant awareness of love, of light and of service. He further explains that in this dimension simply thinking of something creates it immediately. From the perspective of guides all entities, including us humans, are part of the oneness – Ortan sees us as divine sparks of energy, each with a unique role to play in the evolution of the universe. He reminds us that we all come from the divine source and in time we will all return to it. Furthermore, the main experience of the divine is love and light – the vibrations that are always present in the guide's dimension of reality.

Ortan explains that you could visualize reaching the guide's dimension as going through many layers or planes, each of which is energetically different. This is just like the experience of death, where souls pass first to the astral plane and then onwards and upwards. At death, of course, we are assisted by some of the souls already on the other side: they help to lift us to the level that is appropriate for us.

When I begin to channel Ortan I first feel a sense of his love, and then as he moves in to share energy with me there is a slight shift in my body, as if I have just rocked very slightly forwards. Once we have merged I feel tremendously expanded, loving, patient and tranquil. As I channel I just move out of the way and let Ortan do the talking. I don't hear him – I just find that I can start talking and he is doing that talking. I don't need to think about it or monitor it at all. It is as if I am in a state of meditation. Although I can hear what is going on if I choose to, I rarely take that option.

Shalaya's energy is completely different from that of Ortan. I can only describe it as feeling 'larger' than Ortan's and more intense. His voice is a little deeper than Ortan's and he tends to talk a little more slowly. When I channel Shalaya I feel the love and expansion just as I do with Ortan, but Ortan has a sense of humour and fun that is not really present in my experience of Shalaya, who feels much more focused. People who are present when Shalaya is channelled report that there is a very different sensation for them too – they say Ortan is more 'grounded', more interested in mundane, earthly matters, than Shalaya. Shalaya's energy is quite difficult to hold, as he seems more 'alien' than

Ortan in a sense. Unlike Ortan, Shalaya has no interest in subjects such as physical health – he doesn't work with me for channelled readings as Ortan does, but only joins me when I am teaching advanced students. He describes himself as a focus of vibration; he says he is a being of light and vibration, with no form and no physical existence. From Shalaya's perspective the world of matter is a tricky place – he has great sympathy with us and the suffering that we experience in the human form. He explains that he is not bounded by space, time, matter or any other aspects of a physical environment; in fact he has told me that he does not have independent existence in the way that we have. Although he is an identifiable energy, his type of beings just project their consciousness out across time and space in order to communicate with us. When asked about his name, Shalaya just said that this is of no importance – the word 'Shalaya' represents his frequency (see p.22), but he is neither male nor female. But I always refer to Shalaya as 'he', since 'it' somehow doesn't feel right in our language.

Personal guides

Everyone has a personal guide. This is why everyone who wants to is able to channel. These personal guides are here specifically to assist you in fulfilling your higher purpose in this lifetime. Your personal guide will be interested in the things that you are interested in and will be able to advise you on your personal life, your career, your relationships, your health – whatever you want to ask about. These personal guides work to help you throughout your life, focusing on you as an individual (for a channelling on personal guides see p.127).

In my work with Ortan I have been constantly amazed by how easy it is for people to channel. It is as if these personal guides are just one step away from our waking consciousness, ready and willing to work with us.

Transcension guides

Ortan describes himself as a transcension guide – these are guides whose primary focus is on our growth and our ascension into ever higher levels of spiritual awareness (for a channelling on transcension guides see p.127).

Ortan says that some apparent guides are not true guides but our higher selves. He goes on to explain that we can channel our higher selves or guides or both if we so choose. At the beginning of your growth, channelling the higher self is a very useful thing; I did this myself in my early years of channelling. Once you are channelling you can ask: are you a guide or are you my higher self?

It will be helpful at this point to distinguish between the higher self, the soul and the monad. You can see them as parts of yourself that exist at different levels.

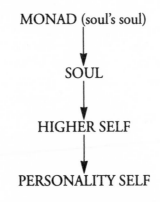

MONAD (soul's soul)

↓

SOUL

↓

HIGHER SELF

↓

PERSONALITY SELF

Ortan defines transcension as ascending and transcending the bounds of present reality and transmuting it into a different kind of reality. He has also made it clear that the process of ascension is currently taking place for all humanity and for our planet. This is discussed in Chapter 2.

Healing guides

Many healers are drawn to learn to channel. When working with them in classes it often becomes clear that they have been channelling their guide or guides for a long time, but they were not conscious channels – they didn't realize where the energy was coming from or how to access it at will. There are many healing guides now and there will be a great need for healing as we take more and more responsibility for our own health at all levels – physical, mental and emotional.

Healing guides are often not verbal guides. They work with colour and energy, with frequencies and vibrations, and don't normally need to use words with those who are working with them. The partnership or relationship between a healing guide and a healer is more of an intuitive thing. This is why healers often have more than one guide. Healing guides can channel through particular rays or particular frequencies (see p.22) for particular things. They work on different frequencies, and combined will produce a different effect.

Ortan says that all healing comes from the divine level, the All That Is. We therefore don't heal people but are just the channels for healing energy (for a channelling on healing see p.128).

Learning to channel is one way to become a more effective healer, and this will be discussed in more detail in Chapter 8. If you are a healer, channelling on the current state of energy of your clients is extremely useful both to them and to you. Many homeopaths, spiritual healers, osteopaths and other alternative healers have found their guide's assistance invaluable in their practice. One acupuncturist has found that her guide will help her word her suggestions in such a way that their impact is greatly enhanced. As a result, it is much more likely that her clients will follow her advice.

Healing guides are often angels (see below), and they are one of the easiest types of guide to contact. The angels of love and healing work through healers, and those healers who are conscious channels can easily have a direct experience of loving assistance of these beings in their work. In short, healers who also channel experience a richness and confidence in their work that develops and deepens as they continue.

Creative guides

There is a whole level of guides who are to do with creating things: they create music, art, environments and much more.

Many people channel these creative guides or master builders – whatever you wish to call them.

People who work in the arts or other creative fields will fall into a reverie; this is when they connect with their creative guides. Much of the work which we consider inspirational comes from guides such as this, who are on a very pure frequency. Their channel has chosen to incarnate and to hold this pure frequency in this particular lifetime.

Clearly the artistic and creative guides are completely aligned with the higher purpose of the channel. From my own observations and with Ortan's guidance, I have come to believe that the most creative among us are also natural channels. There are many stories about composers who 'hear' fully formed the music they go on to write. There are also stories of information coming to both artists and scientists through dreams. Perhaps the best-known concerns the discovery of the structure of DNA, the substance which transmits genetic information from one generation to the next. In a dream one of its discoverers, Crick, 'saw' the distinctive double helix shape of its molecule. He was subsequently able, in a waking state, to use this inspirational dream to move his scientific work forward.

Angels

Each angel vibrates only to its particular frequency. As an analogy, one could imagine them holding on to slivers of light which have the frequency of joy, healing, love, abundance and so on. In any channelling class of around twenty-five people at least one or two will be channelling angels.

Angels are usually channelled by people as a preparatory stage to open their hearts and to bring some joy and lightness into their lives, for they work from the heart as all guides do. Often their very lightness is enough to open the person's energy enough to be able to hold a guide (some people are unable to hold a guide energy at the beginning). The angels are also extremely interested about what is happening on the earth plane. Angels are completely aligned to service. Channelling for this book on 10 August 1995, Ortan said: '*It is service they seek out as a bloodhound seeks out its quarry.*'

As explained earlier, angels often choose to channel through people who are healers or who need healing. They often come in for a short time to prepare the channel's energy for the next guide, especially if the person channelling has not had much experience with meditation and energy work. Because angels hold a pure frequency they are very useful for those who need more discipline or who are looking for their higher purpose or trying to find their higher path of growth.

An angel called Samuel, channelled by a friend, Jennie, assisted me in writing this book (see p.129). His channelling was accompanied by a deep feeling of love and of a form of purity and innocence that was truly beautiful to experience. Often angels will connect with us without our realizing what is happening. We will simply experience feelings of great joy, of opening, of hope or of love – these are the sorts of emotions that characterize angelic contact. As we learn to quieten our minds, so we can open more and more to the whispers of these wonderful beings.

Guide names

People are always interested in the names of guides. They ask in classes, and in readings too people often enquire of Ortan what the name of their guide is. Ortan always says that the name is of no importance: you can perceive the name as being like a call signal on CB radio – a way of tuning in to the unique energy signature of your guide. When my guide Shalaya was asked why he introduced himself by that name he said: '*We are all one being, and "I as Shalaya" simply reflect a particular energy frequency and so I identify this frequency as Shalaya, for this frequency best reflects my/our energy.*'

Sometimes, even after successfully channelling their guide, people have no clear idea of the guide's name. But this really doesn't matter – it is the connection that is important. Some people in our classes get no name at all, but have no difficulty in channelling. So if you find that you cannot get a name when you begin to channel don't worry, but just enjoy the connection.

Below, in no particular order, are some guide names taken from classes over the years.

Examples of guide names

White Cloud	Running Water	White Eagle
Voltan	JK	Chimal
Ashtar	Yarwey	Zortan
Havar	Pal	Sovar
Sapphire	Ortala	Orteya
Hamar	Zena	Lyria
Serang	Orshala	Melchior
Michael	Raphael	St Germaine
Dyasha	Gornash	Chiron
Armjia	Christos	Olithia
Guy	Skysos	Light Angel
Korei	Omar	Michael
Micael	Jahal	Rockie Bear
Tibius	Islan	Shaeya
Aun	Rohan	Yashan
Auriele	Jai	Coerdelia
Amatreya	Ozo	Dwal Khul
Moona	Sananda	Silver Haven
Evis	Simone	Tadeus
Autis	Islis	Nemoho
Dibdin	Sabu	Jonathan
Ottila	Oran	Muburek
Tanqui	Iabo	Ranthea
Quick Silver	Chaim	Ocara
Adran	Chan	Sorhas

The names of guides don't seem to correlate much with what they are here to do with you, or with how they are going to help you. You will notice that lots of these names are unusual, even weird, but many people channel guides with perfectly ordinary names like John, Samuel or Sarah.

There are groups of guides and groups of angels and they often give the same name: the Michaels are an example. Many people channel a guide called Michael, and it is my belief that these are a group of high-level beings who just use one name. There are also other beings you can channel, among them the ascended masters such as Sananda, the ascended Christ.

When people first make the connection with their guide in our classes, they often think they are channelling Ortan. He explained this to me as follows: Ortan is a teacher, and he facilitates the connection between the channel and their guide until it is stabilized. Because he is holding the energy for this connection, the channel tunes into his energy and thinks he/she is going to channel Ortan. Once the connection to their own guide is stabilized, they realize they are not.

Ortan and I have agreed that he will not be channelled by anyone else during my lifetime. If you are using this book to make the connection with your guide, you too may think that you are making a connection with Ortan. You are, but only in the sense that he is out there in the higher realms ready and willing to assist you in making the connection with your own guide. All you need do is ask him to do this in meditation, and the connection will begin to be built. It is not chance that you have been drawn to this book. Ortan has put out the call on the inner planes of reality to all those who can benefit from a connection with him, and you have answered that call.

2

WORKING WITH ENERGY

*Learn to love that critical judgemental part of the
mind and show it other ways to be.*

ORTAN

THE NATURE OF THE UNIVERSE AT AN ENERGY LEVEL

When you connect with your guide, you are connecting with a
being whose existence does not depend on physicality. Guides
often talk about energy and energy work – Ortan discusses our
physical universe in terms of energy as well, and stresses the
importance of the concepts of frequency and vibration.

Frequency and vibration

Ortan believes that the only distinction between us and the
guides is the rate at which we are vibrating. In his experience
frequency is the only thing that is different. He says that our
universe is made up of energy and this energy varies across the
dimensions. The energy vibrates at different frequencies, so by
changing frequencies you change the physical matter in due
course – as above, so below. However whilst energy work may
take only a moment, it can take a while for the effects to come all
the way down through the levels and actually cause a change at
the physical level of experience. We are only equipped to sense
certain frequencies, limited as we are by the sensory apparatus of
the body. However, through work like spiritual development,

channelling and meditation we can start to develop the ability to sense much more subtle energetic differences. Ortan says that we are starting to be able to perceive other, subtler dimensions – as indeed we do when we work with guides.

It is because everything is vibrating at a particular frequency that energy work can take place. For example, when you are channelling healing energy you are bringing through a certain frequency of energy that sets up a resonance. The client then vibrates at that frequency – a frequency that assists them in creating good health. Music/sound and colour therapies work on similar principles – you set up a resonance, and then the body can change its own vibratory rate to match the healing vibration.

Earth, sun and moon

From the guide's perspective, the earth itself has a particular vibratory rate (which Ortan describes as its song), as does the sun. Ortan argues that the sun is a signal of the presence of humans and intelligence, and reminds us of the importance of solar energy to all life forms. It is solar energy that guides use when they move from their frequency to ours, and it is the sun that draws attention to us from other entities and life forms far out in space. Ortan describes the solar vibration as one of light and growth, whereas the frequency of the earth is more that of love. The moon also has its own 'song' – one that is finer and subtler. One of the closest ways in which humans can appreciate this sense of vibration is through instrumental music, song and chanting – through sound we can actually change our consciousness.

Planes and dimensions

Ortan, channelling in 1995, said: *'There are different planes wherein dwell different levels of being, although it is wrong to assume that everything is ordered and hierarchical.'* Guides seem to be quite amused at our constant search for hierarchies and order, and after a while Ortan told me something of how the planes and dimensions are put together. First, of course, there is the earth plane where we live. Then there is the astral plane, much of which is created from the earth plane level. Ortan has warned me frequently that it is extremely important to work with the mental body – the thoughts – because our thoughts at the astral level can create astral energies (for a channelling on this see p.141).

Other dimensions, other entities

In our universe we human beings live in the third dimension, which is bounded by space and time. We are physical beings, and our experience of physicality is paramount in our perception of reality at any one time. Our experience is strongly affected by our physical senses – what we feel, see, touch, taste and smell.

However, there are also other dimensions which contain other beings or entities. The presence of these entities has been documented throughout the centuries in religious and mystical writings. Many mediums and psychics work with what is known as the astral plane, which is close to our own reality but is not physical. There are further planets that continue in ever finer frequencies. Ortan has said that he lives in a dimension of light.

Awakening to the seven dimensions

I believe that we are all souls in physical bodies who have chosen to manifest on the earth plane at this time, but many of us have forgotten who and what we really are. In Gurdjieff's terms, as I have mentioned, we are asleep. In *The Complete Ascension Manual* Joshua Stone explains this process very clearly, talking about the seven dimensions that we are working through, in the following order, in our time on the earth plane:

1. The physical plane.
2. The astral plane.
3. The mental plane.
4. The Buddhic plane.
5. The atmic plane.
6. The monadic plane.
7. The logoic plane.

We can stay asleep for many lifetimes and then eventually begin to awaken. At this point we become spiritual aspirants starting to develop mastery on the physical plane. This is the first level. Then we begin to gain mastery over our emotions and desires; this

LOGOIC PLANE
Seventh initiation
Far beyond normal comprehension. The aspirant merges
with the Planetary Logos.

MONADIC PLANE
Sixth initiation
All bodies merge together. The aspirant usually ascends now
and becomes a being of pure light.

ATMIC PLANE
Fifth initiation
Soul and monad merge into one.

BUDDHIC PLANE
Fourth initiation
Work is now at a soul level. It is unusual to achieve this level
without many lifetimes of work. The heart opens fully and
the aspirant becomes a Lord of Compassion.

MENTAL PLANE
Third initiation
At this level mastery means that we control all aspects of the
personality, mental, emotional and physical.

ASTRAL PLANE
Second initiation
The dimension where we master our emotions and desires.

PHYSICAL PLANE
First initiation
Normal, everyday reality. As we awaken we become
spiritually aware and begin to move along our path
of growth.

Ascending through the Seven Dimensions

represents the second initiation, the astral plane. Mastery of the mental body and therefore over the whole personality (physical, emotional and mental) represents the third initiation. Now, the initiate can build the causal or soul body and gain liberation from the endless cycle of birth and death and rebirth. At the next level the soul body burns up and the soul is absorbed back into the monad (the soul's soul) and the monad becomes the guiding principle. At this point the person is a Lord of Compassion, sometimes known as an arhat. This is the fourth initiation.

At the fifth initiation there is a merging with the monad, and at the sixth all bodies are transformed into light as the monad descends completely and merges with the physical level. This leads to the process which Stone calls Ascension. Now the initiate has the choice of staying on the physical plane to continue his or her path of service to humanity, or returning to the spiritual world. At the seventh initiation the initiate merges with the will of the Planetary Logos (the spiritual Lord of the World and highest being in our planetary system, also known as Sanat Kumara). This is the highest level of initiation possible on the earth plane.

This movement through the planes as described by Stone is carried out through meditation and spiritual practices. Guides exist at high levels of evolution – at least the fourth dimension and above. But remember that this is just one way of making sense of dimensions. Many guides do not consider such delineations either important or useful – but I believe some delineations help us to make sense of how we move on a path of growth.

Thought creates reality

We create our own reality. Ortan explains that if each of us tries to keep our thoughts and our emotions positive, together we can create a different, and truly magical, reality. What we focus on is what we increase, so it is extremely important to keep a positive focus – a focus on the high and the good. By doing this we help to counteract negative thought forms. This understanding means that we can create an ever more beautiful reality in our lives on the earth plane. Ortan points out that there is an interaction between the thought forms that we create at the astral level and the creation of our lives on the earth plane. The thought forms that are created on the astral plane last a long time before they dissolve.

When we are channelling, then, we need to go up through the astral plane, keeping our thoughts clear and positive, for by the law of attraction we draw to us that which vibrates at a similar frequency, and this is especially true at the lower levels of vibration. The guides are found in a much higher dimension or frequency, to put it another way, than the astral plane.

No time, no polarities

Where the guides are there is no concept of time. Although we talk about going up through the dimensions, Ortan stresses that this too is an incorrect description. Actually, everything is woven together.

Realizing that time is just something that exists at our level of reality creates some interesting possibilities. As Ortan remarks, it means that we can access the future just as easily as we can access the past – in fact, at higher levels no differentiation is made.

Just as there is no time, so there is no polarity in the higher realms. All the differentiations we so love to make – black/white, male/female, high/low – just don't seem to exist for guides.

Our perception of guides' energies

Ortan is often asked about what he is doing, where he is and what he, and other guides, look like. He understands that this is of great interest to us. Once he took me to 'see' where he dwelt; to me it looked like a vast white cavern filled with blinding white light which was strangely moving. When he is asked if we will eventually inhabit the dimension he lives in, he says that when we die we do rise up through the planes and we certainly do have the potential to become inhabitants of these wonderful levels of reality so filled with the light of love and service.

As to what Ortan looks like, to me he is just a brilliant white light whilst Shalaya looks rather like a collection of starry points of light. One friend told me that her guide 'appears to me as wispy forms of light coming together to create the most delicate flowing material you can imagine'. Another said that 'Running with

Water is male and looks like a very strong Indian Chief,' and a third that 'She is slender with milk-white skin and long black hair. I cannot identify features – she is Light.' What Ortan does stress about this is that we are bounded by our limited sensory perceptions, and we only experience a very small part of the guide's energy.

Discipline and integrity

When discussing thoughts, Ortan emphasizes the concepts of discipline and integrity. 'Discipline' here means control – as you create your own reality, it is important that you are careful about what you create. This links in with integrity. When Ortan talks about integrity he is talking about acting in such a way that you bring no harm to others.

Discipline is something that we need to develop – for example the discipline to meditate regularly, to be careful about our thoughts and actions so that we act mindfully, trying all the time not to hurt others but to aid them. For it is through our thoughts and actions that we create our own 'karma', the accumulation of debts and credits in each lifetime. Through the discipline of meditation we can come to move easily into a harmonized space where we can be in direct contact with higher aspects of ourselves. Once we can maintain that contact, it is easy to live with integrity from a higher place of awareness. Ortan is very clear that meditation is all-important in the development of both discipline and integrity. From the space created by meditation we can reflect on our actions and learn to control our thoughts.

Ortan repeatedly stresses the importance of the development of the concepts of cooperation, caring and nurturing so that we can create a world filled with goodwill for all. He also often discusses the importance of letting go of judgements of others and accepting them for who they are, with unconditional love.

THE ENERGY OF LOVE AND SELF-LOVE

Working with guides brings a new and deeper understanding of love. To be a good channel you will need to open up to love and especially to self-love. Love is the energy that can transform negativity and change the way that you think to support your growth and that of those around you. Moving to a love-centred consciousness releases you from being so centred in the head and enables you to become centred in the heart.

Just sit for a moment before you read on about love and think about where you experience your consciousness. Close your eyes and feel where in the body you feel the focus of your consciousness. Is it your head? Many of us become so absorbed in the 'busyness' of our everyday lives that we lose touch entirely with that genuine part of ourselves that is loving, accepting and joyous.

Love begins with self-love. This concept is very difficult for the large numbers of us who have been taught to put others first, and it tends to get confused with ideas of selfishness or egoism. Remember the safety routines on planes – when the oxygen masks drop, you are instructed to put on your own mask first and then to assist others. Love works in a similar way. Only when you love and accept who you are, are you in a good enough position to do the same for others. Ortan says: *'Learn to love that critical judgemental part of the mind and show it other ways to be. So also practise loving the thoughts and loving all aspects of the personality. You may even wish to love yourself in the future and in the past. And send love back to yourself and forgive yourself in the future and in the past for all that you have done.'* This doesn't mean that you don't continue to work to be a better person, of course, but it does mean that you learn to stop criticizing yourself and focus properly on that work instead of just thinking about it.

Self-love also means being honest with yourself; not deceiving yourself by pretending to be nicer than you really are, and coming to know yourself fully. Finally, self-love means taking care of your body – not out of vanity, but because the body is the means by which you stay in this experience and are able to learn the lessons your soul chose for this lifetime. So care over diet and exercise are vital (for a channelling on this subject see p.130). Tuning in to the body is an extremely helpful practice – just spend a few minutes each day letting your body have a voice and listen to what it actually needs.

CHANNELLED MEDITATION FROM ORTAN:
OPENING TO LOVE

Find a comfortable, warm place. It is probably best to be
seated with your back upright in a straight-backed chair. To
make sure that you won't be disturbed, take the phone off the
hook or put on your answering machine, and ask any other
people in the house not to interrupt you whilst you are
meditating. After a while you will find it easier and easier to
meditate where you are. . . .

Take a couple of deep breaths into the lower abdomen.
Allow your energy to become more and more harmonized.
Become more and more relaxed as you start to notice the
increase in light with your inner sensing. Take a few minutes
now to relax and open the physical body, letting all the
muscles soften and relax. (*5 minutes*)

Begin to feel light all around you, above you a golden ray
of light shining down into the heart. Let your heart drink in
this light and begin to soften and to heal in this light. (*5
minutes*)

Focus on your breathing now. Breathing in light and
breathing out the pain in your heart, breathing in light and
breathing away sadness. Do this a few times, just letting the
painful emotions be released into the light. (*5 minutes*)

Begin to see your heart centre as a beautiful flower
opening petal by petal, and as it opens notice the light that is
hidden within. Let this light shine out, the light that has
been covered by pain and by sadness, by the negative
emotions of anger and jealousy, greed and hatred. Let this
light dissolve all these negative emotions now.

Resonate to these tender frequencies of love now. It is
through these frequencies that all is accomplished on the
earth plane. Notice the serenity and harmony of this place
now. Notice all the equilibrium within your own spirit and
spend a moment to reach up to the Solar Logos, thanking
that great energy for the gift of life upon the earth plane,
becoming the energy of gratitude. For it is only through this
source of all life that you as souls were able to effect this

miracle of manifestation. And it is through this energy that you can manifest anything you wish, so long as the request is made with a heart that resonates in pure love, and this is the greatest secret of all.

We ask that you tune into these frequencies as often as you can remember. For you can see what they do for your own energy, reaching higher and higher through all the planes of beauty, through all the levels of joy. Your heart must be pure and all else will be given to you. We send you our love and our light, we send you frequencies of harmony. . . .

That is the basic process of the love meditation. And you will notice that once this meditation is stabilized the thoughts are softened and changed. You may start to see many colours in the state of consciousness that is created by this particular energy shift. Breathing, noticing the softening of the thoughts if there are any. Feeling the adjustment in the heart.

3

PREPARING TO CHANNEL

In order to recognize the type of being that you truly are, it is important to know exactly what it is that you are.

ORTAN

In the next few pages I am going to talk about some of the things that I and my students have found particularly important in being a good, clear channel. You don't have to master them all at once, but you may find this a useful place to begin to prepare to channel.

MEDITATION

Probably the most challenging aspect of channelling is being sensitive enough to distinguish between your own energy and that of your guide. Once the connection is established this is easy to do, but at the beginning, especially if you are working on your own, it can be tricky. To be a really good channel you need to step aside and let the guide do the talking. Of course, your guide will feel like you to some extent, because guides use your body to ground their energy and your body has its own energy signature. You have spent many years in this body and you are familiar with its energy patterns, so it is not surprising that at first it may feel strange to open up to the guide's unfamiliar energy.

It helps to spend some time in meditation practice so that you are clear about who *you* are and the types of thoughts *you* have.

This may sound odd, but through the observation of yourself in this way you get to know the characteristics of your own patterns of thoughts and feelings. You will then be absolutely certain which thoughts are your own and which come from your guide.

Focus and concentration

To channel for a period of time you will need to hold a steady focus and maintain the clear channelling connection with your guide. To develop this ability to focus and concentrate, meditation will be your easiest route. When we teach channelling we send out meditation tapes for our students. One of these tapes contains a series of exercises in focus and concentration; the technique is explained below.

MEDITATION:
FOCUSING ON A SOUL QUALITY

You might like to play some gentle music, light a candle and some incense. Settle into a straight-backed chair with your feet firmly on the floor.

Spend a few minutes relaxing your body, finding a comfortable position in which to meditate and just focusing on the breath. Concentrate your attention on the movement of your breath in and out of the body, letting this take up as much of your attention as you can. Observe the in breath and the out breath, noticing how they are different, noticing their qualities, perhaps observing the expansiveness of the out breath.

When you are calm and centred, maybe five or ten minutes later, start to bring your mind to a soul quality that you would like to develop and experience more. Some suggestions are: peace, tranquillity, self-love, compassion, patience, kindness, unconditional love and courage. Spend some minutes now thinking about that soul quality, seeing yourself filled with that quality, seeing how that might transform your life and your experience. Really focus in on that soul quality and nothing else, letting the thoughts and feelings flow until you start to feel that you have that quality right now and until you are really experiencing it. Then bring yourself back to the room. . . .

You may notice that it is quite hard at first to keep your mind centred on just the one thing. If your mind wanders, and it almost certainly will, don't worry – just gently return your mind to the focus you have chosen. Be kind and gentle with yourself; it takes time to develop focus. Let this form of meditation be a regular practice and you will reap rich rewards. You will develop your ability to focus, but also by the law of attraction you will begin to experience your chosen quality in your life more and more.

Other benefits

Regular meditation offers other benefits too for a channel. Those who regularly meditate can reach a balanced state of awareness very easily; they know how to calm themselves down, how to maintain a state of emotional balance and how to clear their minds. This state of mind is very helpful in channelling. Imagining that the mind is like a smooth lake in which the energy impulses of your guide can be reflected will give you an idea of the state of mind you need to reach to be a good channel. If your mind is in turmoil with your own thoughts, it can be very difficult for the guide to get through to you and for you to distinguish your thoughts from the guide's messages. You could perceive your own thoughts as interference, like the crackle you get from the radio when you haven't tuned into the station properly. Channelling is like tuning in to the higher realms; you are the radio through which you tune in, and when you have interference you are making it much harder for your guide to get through to you.

Regular meditation also enables a channel to develop the qualities of compassion and an open heart. If you want to be a channel for others you need to be able to embrace them wholly for who they are, without judgement and with great love. As explained earlier, guides are drawn to those who echo their own energy patterns, and the energy of high-level guides resonates most strongly to the patterns of unconditional love and service to humanity.

To bring through the highest possible guide you need to purify yourself to reach the highest state you can. In *Insight Meditation* Joseph Goldstein wrote about channelling: 'In traditional Buddhist cultures people believe that devas, or celestial beings from higher planes, can work to protect, guide and help us in different situations. The Buddha taught that devas are drawn to us through the power of virtue and loving kindness. As we cultivate and purify our own morality and love, we open ourselves to receive their positive energy and beneficent help.'

These ancient traditions recognize the importance of bringing ourselves to the highest possible state so that we can channel the beautiful energies of high-level beings. Therefore working with high states of consciousness and with light are very good for your own development and for your development as a channel.

Meditation will also help you to work with your ego. It is only too easy for channelling to go to your head, so to speak – channelling does not make you any better or wiser than anyone else, but it can sometimes lead to delusions of grandeur! Through the discipline of meditation you can reach a state of clarity in which you have no illusions about yourself, and from which you will not need to try to prove yourself better than others. Channelling can lead to real humility as you develop the relationship with this beautiful being of light who is free from the illusions of the earth plane. Channelling will lead you to a true freedom of the spirit.

Finally, regular meditation will bring many gifts in your life and will help you to keep your energy clear even if you are channelling for a large number of people every day. A few minutes of meditation is very refreshing and reviving and will bring you back to your own clear centre.

Suggestions for meditation practice

The many types of meditation can be confusing for a beginner. But to begin with, simply sitting each day is enough. It is the discipline of being with yourself for about half an hour a day that will begin to build into a meditation practice. There are many books and teachers available – just choose the one that feels right to you. The important thing about meditation is to do it – not just to think about it or read about it, but actually to sit and do it regularly.

You might like to try these suggestions for meditations to begin with. You can just learn the processes, or perhaps make a tape to listen to. At the School of the Living Light we make many guided meditations which you can buy on tape (see p.158).

The following technique is a very good, simple preparation for channelling. Creating a bubble of light is also a good form of protection in the sense that it helps to keep your energy clear and high, aligning you with the higher light of the universe. During this meditation you are instructed to work with your aura, the energy field that surrounds your body. Imagine that this energy field stretches about two or three feet all around you, maybe in an egg shape. (See p.37 and Chapter 8 for more information on auras.)

MEDITATION:
CREATING YOUR BUBBLE OF LIGHT

Begin by relaxing your body, sitting with your spine very upright or lying down if you prefer. Let all your muscles relax, and check that there are no areas of tension. Check especially for tension in the jaw, the shoulders, the solar plexus and the stomach. When you have done this focus your attention on your breathing. Just notice the breath moving in and out of the body. Notice how many counts it takes for you to breathe in and how many counts it takes to breathe out. Just notice, and keep very focused on the breathing for a couple of minutes. Then add one count to the in breath and one count to the out breath. Let this stabilize for a couple more minutes and then do it again, adding one count to the in breath and one count to the out breath. Again, let this stabilize for another couple of minutes.

Begin to imagine that on each in breath you are reaching up to the higher realms of light and you are breathing in that higher light, and that on each out breath you release that exquisite light into your aura. You are filling your aura with the light of the higher realms, strengthening your own light and beginning to build a connection with the realms in which you will meet your guide. As you breathe in let the breath move deep into your body all the way down into the abdomen and deep into every cell of your body. Imagine that your whole body is filling up with this higher light and you are becoming radiant with light. Your aura is glowing with light and expanding to accommodate so much radiance. Imagine that your aura is like a big, golden bubble of light all around you, protecting you and keeping you safe from any outside influences. Reach up to your soul now and ask your soul to fill this bubble with the light of your higher purpose, your soul's purpose.

Imagine now that this big bubble of light around you is beginning to lift up, lazily rising up into the sky, and you are safe and protected within this bubble. Let yourself float like this for a few minutes. You may like to imagine that you can look out of your bubble and see the clouds around you, the blue of the sky above you, and maybe you can look down and see a beautiful landscape beneath you. Just enjoy this floating and looking, feeling safe and filled with light.

When you are ready, drift back down in your bubble and come back to the time and place of the room you are in, feeling relaxed and invigorated. Take a few moments to reorient yourself to everyday reality. A good way to do this is to have a cup of tea and spend a few minutes outside if possible. If you feel disoriented when you return from meditation, try stamping your feet and pacing up and down, and then have a cup of tea or other hot drink and a snack.

EXPANDING YOUR AURA

Your aura is an energy field that sits around your physical body. Seen clairvoyantly, the aura is usually composed of beautiful colours that cocoon the body in light. All living things have an aura from which they can draw energy. The aura can be worked with to improve your levels of energy, to clear you of unwanted energy and to shift unwanted symptoms when you begin to channel.

Expanding your aura is a very useful process when you are

tense, stressed, worried, frightened or cross. At such times you tend to shrink your aura, which can give rise to effects such as tension headaches. But expanding your aura will make it easier for you to relax the physical body, and can alleviate headaches and tension. These headaches can also come about because your aura is not big enough to accommodate all the energy you are holding.

Guides, too, have auras – in fact you could say they are really all aura as they are essentially energy beings without physical form. When you channel your guide you merge auras – you could almost say that you take on the energy of your guide. When you are in the higher realms and you first start to get close to each other, you may experience your guide in many ways. Each guide–channel partnership is different, because each guide and each channel is an individual. However, all guides are big! It is useful to learn how to expand your aura and practise this before you actually channel. Otherwise, when you come back from being with your guide you may experience physical problems such as a headache or aches elsewhere in the body. The process is described below and is also available on tape (see p.158) as a meditation led by Ortan.

MEDITATION: EXPANDING YOUR AURA WITH THE LIGHT OF THE HIGHER REALMS

Sit quietly in your usual meditation posture, and make sure that you will not be disturbed for a few minutes. You may like to play some gentle music in the background.

Straighten your spine and breathe deeply, taking the breath all the way into the lower abdomen. Spend a few moments relaxing your physical body so that it is comfortable. Let go of your thoughts and allow your emotions to calm down.

Tune in to your energy and imagine that it is becoming very calm and tranquil, as if you are slowing down. Now start to imagine that you are calling light to you so that you are surrounded by a wonderful, clear light. Let yourself enjoy this experience as you sit in the light. Breathe this light in deeply, focusing on your breath. Don't try to control it, just observe and let your breathing deepen. Spend a few minutes just breathing in the light and filling your physical body with the light.

When you feel full of light start to imagine that when you breathe out you are breathing out light and filling your aura with light. Visualize your aura becoming brighter and brighter if you can. It starts to take on a glow. Stay with that experience for a few moments.

Now imagine that with every out breath your aura is expanding. Just as a balloon expands when you blow it up, you are expanding and filling your aura with light. As you do this you may feel very expanded and relaxed, and your breathing may deepen and open up. Just go with your experience, letting your aura continue to expand until you feel a sense of completion.

You may be surprised at how big your aura will become as you do this. Let that be all right. Come back to the room and open your eyes very gently and easily.

Once you have mastered the process of expanding your aura you will be able to do it in an instant – when you are waiting for a train or bus, say, just expand your aura. The more expanded you can keep the aura the better.

PHYSICAL CONSIDERATIONS

Channelling can be physically demanding for the channel. But this does not mean that you cannot channel unless you are physically perfect. However, care and consideration for the physical body are needed. Many people report that, when they first start channelling, their guide's energy is felt in a very physical way, like a strong heartbeat, or a rush of energy through the body, or a strong feeling of emotion. Remember, taking care of your body is at the heart of self-love. Ortan says, channelling for this book on 21 August 1995.

ORTAN: *The nature of love has been taught through the ages by all masters and all enlightened beings. The nature of love begins with love for the organism that you have been gifted to take care of – your body, your brain, and of course your soul and higher self. And it is the starting point for development to come to be easy with this self, this manifested self.*

Ortan stresses over and over again that unless the body is healthy it is very difficult to concentrate on spiritual growth and development. He understands that pain will take over your awareness and exclude many possible states of consciousness, so he works hard to assist people, including me, to be easy with their bodies. I have worried in the past about my weight, as many people do. Ortan says that minor weight gains, which we dislike merely because they make us less attractive, are irrelevant. The only real problem is excessive weight gain, which might affect our health.

Another aspect of physical care is exercise. For the energy to flow easily in the body and to maintain good health I practise yoga, which I find a simple and enjoyable way of keeping fit without stressing the body. You need to find what suits your body best, which may be walking, tai chi, swimming – whatever makes you feel good. Ortan repeatedly stresses that the exercise you choose does not need to be extremely strenuous. In fact he is keen on the gentler forms of exercise, which, he argues, do not lead to a risk of physical injury in the long term. He recommends the practice found in the wonderful teachings of Thich Nat Hanh (see *The Blooming of a Lotus*). A shortened version, which we call Smiling to your Body, is given below.

MEDITATION:
SMILING TO YOUR BODY

Spend a few minutes settling your physical body into a position of comfort. Keep the back very upright but at the same time relax all your muscles.

Now let your breathing settle down to a comfortable rhythm and start to imagine yourself as a five-year-old child.

Now on the in breath see yourself as a five-year-old child and on the out breath smile with compassion to that five-year-old child, actually smile, because the energy of smiling can heal you emotionally and physically. Repeat this step three times.

Aware of your body now, on the out breath smile to your body, your whole body, smiling warmly to your whole body. Repeat three times.

Now as you breathe in become aware of your skin and as you breathe out smile to your skin. Repeat three times.

As you breathe in become aware of your heart. As you breathe out smile to your heart and in your smile feel the energy of gratitude. Give joyous thanks to your heart for all that it does for you every single day of your life. Repeat three times.

As you breathe in become aware of your lungs. As you breathe out smile to your lungs and in your smile feel the energy of thanks, joyous thanks for all that your lungs do for you every single day. Repeat three times.

As you breathe in become aware of your liver. As you breathe out smile to your liver and in your smile feel the energy of thanks, joyous thanks for all that your liver does for you every single day. Repeat three times.

As you breathe in become aware of your stomach. As you breathe out smile to your stomach and in your smile feel the energy of thanks, joyous thanks for all that your stomach does for you every single day. Repeat three times.

As you breathe in become aware of all your internal organs. You don't have to name them all. As you breathe out smile to all your internal organs and in your smile feel the energy of thanks, joyous thanks for all that your internal organs do for you every single day. Repeat three times.

As you breathe in become aware of your whole physical body. As you breathe out smile to your body and in your smile feel the energy of thanks, joyous thanks for all that your body does for you every single day. Repeat three times.

Now imagine that your whole body is drinking in this energy of your genuine smile, and as it does, imagine that your smile and your gratitude are nourishing your body, allowing your body to become more and more relaxed and filled with healing light.

On the in breath imagine that light is filling your body and on the out breath smile to your body and enjoy. Repeat for as long as you wish.

ENERGY FLOWS AND THE CHAKRA SYSTEM

It is helpful for a channel to be aware of the energy meridians in the body and the functioning of what is known as the chakra system (see Chapter 8). If the energy is flowing easily through the meridians, it will be reflected in the flow of the physical body. Blockages will make channelling more difficult for you to do.

These meridians are the channels for the subtle energy, which the Chinese call chi, to move through the body. The meridians are like lines running through the body carrying this chi energy. Kinesiologists work directly with this type of energy, as do acupuncturists. If the chi energy is not flowing properly, ill health will follow.

One of the easiest ways to check if your energy is balanced and flowing is to see a holistic therapist. I visit an acupuncturist four times a year, when the seasons change: after the spring equinox at the end of March, after the summer solstice at the end of June, after the autumn equinox at the end of September, and after the winter solstice at the end of December. These visits keep my chi energy flowing and support my physical, mental, emotional and spiritual well being. Acupuncture is my personal preference, but you must choose the type of approach that feels good for you. For example, Shiatsu too works on the meridian system. Some people prefer the approach of Ayurvedic medicine, which is based on body type and focuses on diet as a way to bring balance to your energy. Reflexology, too, can be very beneficial, again working on the energy balances of the body through pressure points in the feet.

Balancing, aligning and opening the chakras is also important for good energy flow and physical wellbeing. Various exercises and meditations will assist the flow along the chakras. There are many good books which contain information about chakras, and if you are not familiar with this literature you may find it a very interesting part of your training to be a channel to learn about the way in which the chakras influence the flows of energy at every level of your being. Chapter 8 focuses on channelling about the chakras, and the exercises and ideas there may be helpful. At the School of the Living Light we also make tapes to guide you in this work with the chakras (see p.158).

Emotional Factors

While you are distressed or going through an emotionally difficult time, it is probably best not to channel for other people. You might even find it difficult to channel for yourself if you are in a period of emotional upheaval, because your mind will be preoccupied with your difficulties and challenges. It is easiest to channel when you are feeling emotionally balanced. If you know that you have unresolved emotional problems it may be very useful to see a therapist or a counsellor. Your preparation to be a good channel will be greatly enhanced if you face your emotional difficulties and work through them.

This doesn't mean, however, that you have to have your life completely in order at an emotional level – if you did, most of us could never consider being a channel! You will find that your guide will bring a great deal of wisdom through to assist you in the process of making your life work at an emotional level, but your guide will also need you to be committed to clearing your emotional body of any old patterns and difficulties. It is important to remember that you have been born as a human being, with all the challenges that this entails, because your soul chose it. So don't be afraid of emotional challenges – they also bring growth for you.

Affirmations
To help in this process of emotional clearing, try affirmations. Reading inspiring books will also keep your mind focused on

growth when you might be feeling down or discouraged. I have given a few suggestions for affirmations below, but feel free to make up your own according to your own special needs.

AFFIRMATIONS

I love myself just as I am now.

I live in harmony with all the people I know and work with.

I attract loving people into my life because I am open to love and I joyously give and receive love.

I live in the present, giving thanks for all that happens, knowing that it is for my highest good.

I am in the process of making positive changes in my life.

I release the past and I joyously welcome the future.

I am ready to channel a high-level guide.

When you have chosen the affirmations you want to work with, write them down and keep where you will see them during the day – maybe pinned on a noticeboard near your desk, or attached to the fridge door. Whenever you catch sight of them, repeat the affirmations to yourself three or four times. Think a little about what they really mean and how they reflect a truth that you now recognize.

Learning to love

When you open to channel you will find that the experience of your guide is one of unconditional love. If you are unused to love in your life this can be almost overwhelming. It is therefore very helpful to prepare to receive this love and to return it by opening to love in your life right now.

The most important part of loving is to learn to love yourself. When you feel good about who you are, you are able to face problems with ease. Let go of self-criticism and release yourself from other people's opinions about you.

You may be surprised by one aspect of your growth into love – you may need to let go of some of your friends. Some friends can be very draining, so consider them individually and notice how they affect your energy. You may find that you are actually giving away a lot of energy to others, but not getting anything in return. Not only are you not getting anything in return, you are not helping your friends either. If they can always come round to see you and wallow in self-pity or other negative emotional states, they are not learning to cope by themselves with what their lives are bringing them.

Many people who are on a path of spiritual growth are very kind-hearted and generously give their time and energy, but this may not be serving their own growth and ultimately the growth of others. If you have friends who load you with their problems and worries, try to hold them in your heart but stay detached. This doesn't mean that you don't care about them – but don't feed their need to depend on you, which isn't moving them forward. Smile and imagine your bubble of light all around you protecting you from their negative energies and keeping you safe in the light. Stay centred and open-hearted, and leave your friends space to find and develop their own solutions.

SENSING SUBTLE ENERGIES

Learning to channel is a process of learning to sense subtle energies. Meditation will increase your sensitivity greatly, but it can also be helpful to follow some exercises. One way is to spend time with other living organisms such as animals, plants and crystals. You will find that each has its own unique energy structure, which you can actually sense quite easily.

EXERCISE: SENSING SUBTLE ENERGY

Try sensing your house plants or the plants in your garden. Take a plant and sit quietly with it for a few minutes, then move your hand slowly to about a couple of inches away from the plant. You will feel an invisible layer around the plant – its energy field. That feeling may be just a gentle sensation on your palm as you draw your hand towards it, or a tingling. Now just imagine that you and the plant are sharing energy, just being together, and open your mind to the plant's energy. Ask the plant with your inner voice: 'Is there anything you need?' and be very open to hear the reply. Send love to the plant. Don't expect to hear a voice. You may suddenly get the idea that the plant needs repotting or watering or feeding, or maybe you will get the idea that nothing needs to be done right now.

Approach this with a sense of play and openness and see what comes up. You might be surprised!

CHOOSE TO BE A CHANNEL

Begin thinking about how it would be to channel a guide. Channelling will bring you many gifts. Be clear now that this is what you really want and what you are working towards. Tell the universe that you are ready to channel.

To begin the channelling activation and to make a strong connection with your guide, it helps to be very clear that this is what you want to do. In your regular meditations, affirm that you are ready to channel. For example, you could open your meditations by affirming that 'I am ready to be a clear channel for the light' or 'I am ready to channel the highest possible guide'. Let the universe know that you mean it and that you are ready. Spend time in meditation asking for assistance in the opening to channel process, and close your meditations with the affirmation 'I am a channel for the highest possible guide. I ask that this guide be with me.'

Be positive about channelling, read about channelling, talk to channels and use your imagination to envisage all the wonderful changes that channelling will bring to your life.

THE LAW OF ATTRACTION

By the law of attraction you attract to you that which you are resonating to – in other words you are like a magnet, drawing to yourself what you are thinking about and what you are filling your thoughts with. When you are aligned with a reality of unlimited potential you can project this unlimited potential into all aspects of your life. Your aura begins to vibrate with the frequencies you have chosen, and then you become more and more magnetic to those qualities in your everyday life.

It is the same with channelling. If you begin to think about channelling, to read about it and to believe that you will channel, you will begin to create a new reality where you are a channel. You will also begin to attract opportunities for meeting others who are interested in channelling, as well as making it much easier for your guide to connect with you.

If you think, 'Oh, I want to be a channel but I don't think I can do it' you are setting yourself up to fail. Think positively and start to believe that you will channel, and you will be paving the way for a strong, easy connection with your guide.

MEDITATION: TO BEGIN TO ALIGN WITH THE ENERGY OF YOUR GUIDE

There are many beings of light available who will help you in this process. In your daily life you may already be getting promptings from your guide. These may be in the form of sudden insights or intuitions. If you were not ready you would not be following this meditation, for the call has been put out to many, and yet still only a few are open to listen, only a few answer that call to spiritual growth. Each time one does, each time one of you chooses to act on that inner listening, you open the door for many others. You are choosing to work with the higher, finer frequencies of light and energy, and by this choice you make these frequencies more available for others to find.

Learning to connect with guides and angels can help you so much in finding your life's purpose. You may have been feeling an inner call as if you have had a mission upon this earth plane. You may know what this is, or you may only be at the beginning of understanding what your purpose here may be. As you connect with your guide you will gain a deeper understanding of your higher purpose, and together with your guide you will be able to act on this knowledge to bring it into your life and carry it out in service. . . .

Start to bring your attention inward, feeling very focused, very centred and very balanced, feeling so quiet within, letting your body grow comfortable as you begin to lift your mind higher as if you are a bird, flying higher and higher into the light. Your mind is clear, letting go of everyday thoughts so that your mind is clearly reflecting the higher planes of reality. You are feeling more and more calm and centred, your energy is expanding as you begin to lift your energy higher and higher, letting the light flow down into your body, letting your energy take on greater beauty and more light.

Imagining now that sunlight is pouring down all around clearing your energy, beautiful warm golden sunlight, just the right warmth. This light is cleansing your aura, and you are growing lighter and brighter so that you are able to hold more light, to radiate more light. Your aura is growing lighter and more beautiful. Many beings of light are being drawn by your light and your beauty. They are here to assist you in moving into the realms of light, the realms of the guides. Ask for the highest possible guide, your guide, to begin the process of opening your energy, to start to establish the link between you more strongly. You do not need to know how to do this. Your guide knows exactly what to do. Simply be open to receive and to allow your guide to make these energy adjustments.

This is a very special time upon the earth plane. Humanity is in the process of a great transformation, and the doorway between the dimensions is more open now than it ever has been and it is easier now than ever before to reach upward. Your guide will help you in many ways in making this connection.

Drinking in the light here, feeling so integrated, so balanced and so safe within your own being. And as you begin to open your heart, feel what a loving, caring person you are. Your ability to love will become stronger and clearer within you as you make the connection with your guides and with higher beings of light, for guides work in the frequencies of love and light and you are now opening yourself to these frequencies in yourself and in your life.

And sitting very comfortably right now and relaxing even more deeply, imagine and begin to sense and to feel the guides and beings of light who are assisting you in this process of opening as they gather about you. You might feel surrounded by a circle of light, just letting yourself be very open to the light and the love of the higher realms and of your guide. Your guide has been waiting for you to reach up and to choose to channel and to connect with the higher realms. Ask your guide now to begin to strengthen and to deepen the connection between you. You may not be conscious of this process at all – that is fine. Ask your guide to assist you in releasing any thoughts that do not serve you on this path of growth, to assist you in letting go of the negative thoughts, the doubts and the fears, so that you may grow in joy and in peace with a heart full of compassion and love. And ask your guide to help you in following the highest possible path of growth, making choices that are high and wise, making choices that serve your growth and are aligned with the integrity of your being.

Stay in this space with your guide for as long as you wish. When you are ready to come back, thank your guide and all the beings of light who have been assisting you and slowly start to imagine that you are drifting down through the light back into your body. Take a few moments to stretch and re-orient to the room.

Take your time as you work through the suggestions in this chapter; there's no rush. A thorough preparation for channelling will make the actual move into being a channel much easier. In the next chapter we will look at ways of protecting yourself as a channel, and in the chapter after that we shall be looking at opening the connection with your guide(s) so that you can verbally channel their wisdom.

4

PSYCHIC PROTECTION AND CLEARING

For it is very easy now to become bound up in the frequencies of fear, and we say to you that there is nothing to be fearful about – all fear begins within. Remember always that where there is light there can be no darkness. Work to increase your light and you will free yourself from fear.

ORTAN

In almost every channelling class we have taught, people have asked whether it is necessary to protect themselves – to keep their energy clear of the influence of others. You will find that learning to take care of yourself at every level is a very good way to develop self-love, which is the key to protection.

There is no such thing as negative energy, only energy you cannot yet handle.

Ortan and I have developed our own approaches to protection, and they are simple to use. There are two stages: the first is to clear your energy of negative influences, and the second is to stay clear once you have done so. Both these techniques are available as guided meditations from the School of the Living Light (see p.158). You do not need to be able to channel to follow our angel meditations: calling on the assistance of the angels is one of the most powerful ways to keep your energy clear and sparkling with light.

Clearing your Energy, Cleansing your Aura

The most direct way to clear your own energy is to work with the angels of purification and your guide. These angels are in service to humanity and will help you to release negative energies from your aura.

Meditation: Clearing your Energy with the Angels of Purification

Find a quiet place where you will not be disturbed for a few minutes. You may like to burn incense or perhaps aromatic oils to clear the environment around you and to help the angels come easily to you. Settle down into a meditative position with your back straight and call in your guide. If you wish, get some friends together so that one of you can read the meditation out loud for the others. If you are on your own you can just read through the meditation and try to imagine as much as you can of the description given. This meditation is available on our tape set *Gifts from the Angels* (see p.158). . . .

Take a couple of deep breaths into the abdomen, breathing in light, and as you are breathing in this light let go of any thoughts, let go of any worries, let go of any tensions so that your body is becoming relaxed, safe and comfortable, freeing you to play in the energy with the angels.

You are going to play with the angels, those beings of light who are so closely connected with the energy of the divine, the Creator. These beings of light are here to assist us in every aspect of our spiritual growth and in every aspect of our everyday lives. All we need to do is to be open to their beautiful energies. Start to imagine that your energy is becoming very beautiful, starting to call light to you. You are filling up with light. You are becoming light.

Spend a moment now to send away any energies that are not your own, releasing them to return to their rightful place in the universe, and calling all your own energy back to you wherever it may be scattered. Calling it back so that you are whole and complete, very balanced, and as you do this you feel stronger. Many times in your everyday life on the earth plane you will collect energies that are not yours. In the process that we will now follow you will be able to release all these energies. You will be able to clear your aura and to let go of grasping or holding on to influences that are not going to contribute to your growth and to your joy.

Continue to call light to you. Fill up with light, feeling more and more peaceful. With your inner sensing you may have a sense of a dancing energy being drawn towards you, perhaps just catching it at the corners of your inner vision. You may see or sense flames or dancing lights. You may see tiny forms of exquisite human shapes, you may see sparkles of colour as you and your guide call in the angels of purification. Allow the angels to move closer and closer to you. Open your heart, affirm to the angels: 'I am ready to release all influences and energies that do not contribute to my highest good.' As you make this affirmation, open your heart to allow the angels to start to move into your energy so that they are at the edges of your aura.

You may notice an increase in light, you may see colours, you may have a slight tingling sensation in the hands or in the body. Allow it to be as it is, not trying to do anything, noticing the light now as the angels hear your affirmation. Feel the love they are starting to send you as they connect their hearts with yours, sending lines of light, lines of love from their pure hearts to yours, open to receive their love. Feel the beauty and purity of their energy and their joy at being able to work with you, their joy that you are opening to receive their love and their assistance, for all they want to do is help you. It is as if you could say that these angels have a mission in their hearts, a mission of love.

The angels start to fly around your aura. They weave beautiful patterns of light all about you. At first you may just sense this, or you may be able to see this with your inner vision. Be very quiet within now as the angels begin to weave light about you – many, many rainbow colours of light. They are starting to join together now within the weaving of the light and the colour. You are surrounded by a cocoon of rainbow light, and this light is moving into your aura, filling your aura with all the colours of the rainbow. Feel the washes of colour as the angels start to purify and cleanse your aura, strengthening it and preparing you for the final processes of purification.

The angels are gathering together now for the process of purification. They are forming a circle about you. Moving into place as they connect heart to heart with each other. You are in the centre now of this group of angels of purification preparing for the final process. Affirm once more that you are ready to let go of all energies and influences that do not contribute to your spiritual growth. You are ready to let go of all influences and energies that do not take you higher, that do not help you to be a more beautiful and loving person.

The angels are starting to spin about you, forming a continuous circle of light. Slowly at first they are turning, they are catching on to that rainbow weaving that they prepared earlier. That cocoon of rainbow light about you is starting to turn very gently and they are anchoring you now to the planet, sending light down from your base chakra to the centre of this beautiful planet earth. You are secure now, safely connected to the planet.

Imagine that your energy is growing more beautiful. The angels are starting to spin, forming a vortex of rainbow light all about you. Turning, all you can see is spinning colours all about you. You are immersed in spinning colour, and as the angels begin to spin about you, you are forming a vortex of light and this light is rising up all about you. The angels are clearing your energy, purifying your aura, lifting up all influences to the higher realms where all is dissolving in light and you are left with a deep sense of peace. You may have a sense of pure colours as the angels have lifted all influences from your aura. Your aura now is clear and pure, filled with light, filled with all the colours of the rainbow, filled with all potentials for your good and for your growth. Feel the joy that this clarity brings to you, as if your emotions are clear and free. Your body is serene and strong. You are connecting to your path of spiritual growth, of personal growth, connecting to all your potential, all your ability to be strong and pure in the light.

You may feel a sense of tingling in the light now, and the angels start to come back. You notice them once more dancing about you. They are so happy that you have chosen this path of light. Send them your loving thanks and feel their love coming back to you, feel the lightness and purity of your energy. Feel the cocoon of rainbow light that the angels have woven about you to protect you, to assist you in keeping your energy pure and clear. From now on you can always use this process whenever you wish to clear your energy with angels. It is their joy to serve you and to assist you in your growth, and it is our joy to assist you in making that connection with these beautiful light beings. So say farewell to the angels just for now, taking a couple of deep breaths into the abdomen and noticing your energy. You are strong, you are clear, you are focused, you are balanced, you are light. Very gently and easily start to bring your awareness back to the physical body, to the time and the place of the earth plane.

This beautiful meditation will work very well as a method of clearing your energy. If you have trouble visualizing things don't worry – many people only sense the shifts that the clearing brings, while others hardly feel anything. The cocoon of light that the angels weave about you will help to repel negative energies and will last a day or so. After a while you will find that you can easily follow this process whenever you need to.

Another effective way to cleanse your aura involves sun and water. Lying in the sun will cleanse and nourish your aura – though obviously you don't want to risk sunburn, so follow this advice with care. Five minutes is all it takes. Just sitting with your face turned to the sun and your eyes closed is very relaxing and invaluable in clearing your aura. Precede or follow this with a bath in which you have dissolved a handful of Epsom salts or Dead Sea salts and you will be sparkling clean once again. This is a lovely way to end your day.

Building Protection from Negative Energies

It is also important to protect yourself from taking on these negative energies in the first place. You are on a path of spiritual growth and you are a sensitive and caring person, so you may attract people who are not so far along the path of growth as you are. It is a law of the universe that those who are more evolved attract those who are less evolved. You have probably experienced this yourself. Think how good it feels to be with a person who is more spiritually developed than you are – there is a sense of peace, of expansiveness and of happiness. You make your less evolved friends feel like this.

You will attract those who realize, probably at a subconscious level, that just being with you makes them feel better and enables them to release a lot of their negativity around you. Unfortunately you will pick up these negative energies as they move through your energy fields. Eventually, however, you will find that you can transmute any energy that is around you. Call on your higher self and your soul for assistance if you want it – but remember, you have to ask for it.

In the meditation for clearing your energy you will have noticed that at one point you are asked to release any energies that are not yours and to call back all your own energy to you. This simple process is very helpful as a regular practice, enabling you to feel whole and complete, balanced and stronger. It is an excellent way to start your daily meditation session, as you will feel stronger and lighter. You don't need to know where your energy has been scattered, just call it back to you. In the same way, you don't need to know whose energy has been attracted to you, just release it from your aura and let it return to its rightful place in the universe.

When you are channelling for other people it is a very good idea to take a few minutes to centre yourself in your own experience and to clear your energy. After a reading I always clear my own energy just as a precaution. Your guide will protect you whilst you are doing the reading but you also need to learn to take very good care of yourself, this is all part of taking responsibility for yourself.

CLEARING YOUR ROOM OF NEGATIVE ENERGIES

The room in which you meditate, do readings, maybe write your diary and so on would ideally be one in which you did nothing but these high activities. But not many of us can dedicate an entire room like this. The answer is to know how to keep your rooms clear of negative and unwanted energies that are not aligned with your own. It is good practice to do this regularly, about once a fortnight or even more often if you have lots of visitors. Trust your own intuition. There are several techniques that you can use. Those listed below are ones I use myself and have found to be effective.

Crystals in the room

In my workroom I keep a few friendly crystals to help hold the energy steady and to cleanse the energy for me too. Often during readings and healings people release a lot of energy, and the crystals can absorb it for you. A favourite of mine is amethyst: I have a couple of amethyst crystals in the workroom and I cleanse them very frequently (see below). Amethyst transmutes lower energies to higher energies and is a stone of spirituality and peace. It is also said to be useful in protection against psychic attacks by transmuting the energy into positive and loving energy. Clear quartz clusters also seem to be very effective, bringing harmony into your workroom and holding a high, steady energy.

There are three ways of cleansing a crystal. My favourite is to take a good-quality crystal glass bowl, fill it with enough freshly filtered water to cover the crystal, and then add a couple of pinches of sea salt. Place the crystal in the bowl and leave outside for twenty-four hours so that it is exposed to a full cycle of the sun and moon: the best time to do this, if possible, is at the full moon.

Then bring the crystal inside, wash it under running water and polish with dry, lint-free cloth. As an alternative to this some people bury their crystals so that the earth can renew their energy. You can also cleanse crystals using Reiki techniques.

Smudging

Incense is a wonderful cleaning influence in a room. I don't burn incense during readings as some people find it unpleasant, but I do use it to set up the room and to cleanse it afterwards. You can use specially made smudging bundles which are easily available, or you can just use ordinary incense – frankincense is very good. Just light your incense and walk around the room in a clockwise direction. As you do this imagine that all negative and unwanted energies are dissolving in the cleansing smoke.

Oils

Many aromatherapy books are available, giving details of how to use the oils. I use khella in my oil burner for clarity, mint for focus, lavender to cleanse and tea tree to ward off germs. When you are seeing many people they often come with coughs and colds; I find tea tree oil very effective to protect me from infections.

Vortex of light

This meditation can be used to cleanse the energies in a room. It dissolves negative energies in a vortex of light.

Meditation: Clearing your Room with Light

Call in your guide as you move into a meditative state, asking your guide to help you to release any energies that are not aligned with your highest purpose. Call in the angels to assist you as well. Let your own energy become very tranquil and centred.

Begin to imagine that the light of the higher realms is shining down all around you and you are filling up with this light, breathing it deep into your body as it fills every cell of your physical body. Imagine this light radiating out into your aura and then out into the room so that the room is filled with this high light.

Now imagine that all the negative energies that have accumulated here are being filled with light, and that this light is forming into a vortex spinning in a clockwise direction like a small tornado of light. This vortex of light is gathering all the energies that are not aligned with your highest purpose and highest good, and lifting them up into the higher realms so that they may be transmuted and dissolved in the higher light. Continue to do this until you feel quite sure that the cleansing is completed.

Thank the angels and your guide for their assistance before you finish.

Tibetan bells

The little Tibetan bells, which look like two small cymbals on a length of cord or thong, are rung by letting them knock gently against the edges of each other. The sound they produce is very clearing. Crystal healers sometimes use these bells to clear and protect their crystals. They are lovely to use before and after a meditation or channelling. When you are clearing space just walk about with the bells, sounding them in the four corners of the room and anywhere else you feel drawn to. The sound is very calming and beautiful.

Clean regularly

One of the most obvious and effective ways of cleansing rooms is to combine esoteric techniques such as those discussed above with keeping the room scrupulously clean at the physical level. So vacuuming, dusting, polishing and regular airing are also very important. Throw open the windows and let the fresh air clean out the room – sunlight is a very effective cleansing medium. Fresh air recharges the air in the room.

5

THE CHANNELLING ACTIVATION

From our side when a human reaches up to channel, it is almost an irresistible urge to join with that human if that human is right for that particular guide ... we are unable to resist that call to assist because we have already pledged so to do.

ORTAN

MAKING THE CONNECTION WITH YOUR GUIDE

At channelling classes people invariably find that the first time they channel is the most challenging. On subsequent occasions it usually becomes progressively easier.

There are clear stages in the experience of channelling. Usually after the first session people are both exhilarated and very relieved that they really can do it.

What follows is a transcript of a taped discussion with some of my students at an intermediate-level class, which gives a flavour of their experience with channelling. In the interests of confidentiality, I have not given the students their full names.

LITA: What was it like when you first opened to channel?
T: I can do it!

LITA: What was the feeling like when you first contacted the guide?
T: Very natural, a warm feeling.

LITA: What? Physically warm?

J: Yes, warmth in the body.

T: It's like meeting an old friend. Somebody really special.

R: And the depth of love, the quality of love – it's just completely different.

LITA: That's the thing I remember most. It's this incredible love. I mean, I cried my eyes out – did you?

R: Oh yes. I still do.

J: I think I was relieved, too, because I thought I wouldn't be able to do it. So that was another emotion.

LITA: I think everyone who comes to that class . . . they think they are going to be the one . . . everybody else is going to channel and they're not. And then even when they do . . . I think at the beginning . . . what about the doubts – did you have a lot of doubts?

R: It was very helpful when you said you all channelled and that all the guides were present, and then that was a real confirmation. You need to be told at the beginning that actually you are channelling, because there are so many doubts and it's so incredible that you really are. You need to be reminded!

During the first channelling session it is common for channels to cry as the guide comes in – tears not of sadness but of joy, as their heart opens to the almost unbelievable experience of the total unconditional love that their guide has for them. When I teach channelling I insist that, wherever possible, participants tape this and all the subsequent sessions so that they have a record of themselves. Listening to those tapes can be very helpful at the later stages of channelling. You can do this too if you are learning from this book.

    When you choose to channel a guide, at the beginning there is an important stage which we call the activation process. You do not need to attend a class to experience it. The class is a useful place to experience the initial opening to channel: because all the guides are there, along with angels and other beings of light, the energy is very high and it is very easy to channel in those circumstances. But you can learn to channel without other people being present if you want to. On p.158 you will find a contact address for the School of the Living Light from whom tapes are available.

BEGINNING TO CHANNEL

When you are ready to channel there are a few things to bear in mind.

Posture is important

To facilitate the connection with your guide, strengthen your back muscles so that you can sit with a straight back. The easiest way to sit is the Egyptian posture with your back very upright, your shoulders relaxed, your feet planted firmly on the floor and your hands resting on your legs. This is a very stable posture and can be sustained for long periods. Move your head very slightly back and forward until you feel that the area where it joins the top of the spine is open and relaxed. By keeping your back straight you are allowing the energy flows in the body to move without restriction. As the guide connects with you there is often a surge

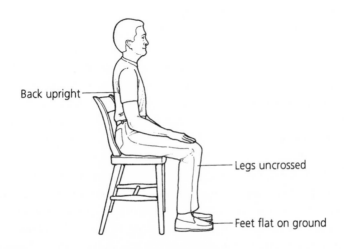

Back upright — Legs uncrossed — Feet flat on ground

The Egyptian posture

of energy, and if you restrict the flow you can set yourself up for lots of physical discomfort – particularly aching shoulders and neck as well as headaches and other minor discomforts. Don't worry too much about this because any discomfort will pass very quickly, but if you want to channel long-term you do need to pay attention to your posture.

Pre-empt interruptions

Put on your answering machine or take the phone off the hook.

Relax and stay calm

When you first channel it is a very exciting experience. Try to stay calm and collected, without any particular expectations. This may be difficult; but the clearer and calmer you are, the easier will be the connection for you and your guide. Let your mind be as clear and as calm as a mountain lake.

Surround yourself with a bubble of light

When you are going to channel, calm your energy, then surround yourself with a bubble of light. Imagine that this bubble is filled with the highest light, the light of your soul, forming a bubble to protect you from any influences that are not aligned with your soul's light and your soul's purpose.

Trust your guide

Guides are very loving and caring, and want to help humanity. If you keep this in mind it helps considerably. Don't try to edit what your guide says – this is a great lesson in trust. Trust the guide to know what the person talking to the guide needs to know.

The high perspective of guides means that they have a much broader, deeper understanding of what to say than we do. We operate in day-to-day reality at the personality level; sometimes this is referred to as the lower self or personality self – you at a normal level of functioning. At a personality level it can be difficult to know what a person needs from a reading, but from the level of the guide everything looks very different. Here is an example.

Ortan and I gave a reading to a well-known television personality, a very attractive, high-powered, dynamic woman whom I shall call Jane here. She had been suffering health problems, particularly with her digestion; because she was a workaholic she was not taking enough rest, not eating properly and driving her physical body into the ground. She was also having relationship problems with her husband.

Within a few minutes of beginning the reading, Ortan told Jane that the root of many of her problems was that she was an alien. I, as my personality self, cringed at hearing this. What would Jane think? Ortan explained that the reason Jane had so much trouble taking care of herself was that she had not had a human body for many incarnations and had absolutely no idea how to take care of it.

After the reading I came back and looked at Jane, who grinned and said she had always known she was an alien! She further told me that she had trouble remembering to eat and a deep belief that she really did not need to sleep or even to rest. Once she understood why she had this belief she was more able to work with her difficulty about being a human being.

If I had edited out the information Ortan had given her about being an alien I would have done Jane a disservice. Ortan knew that she needed to know this; he was right. Over the years that we have worked together Ortan has given me numerous lessons in trust, in letting go and allowing the higher realms to work through me as a channel. The more I have been able to let go, the easier and more joyous my life as a channel has been.

Let the information flow

When you first begin channelling your guide the experience is often overwhelmingly beautiful and you may feel immersed in love, acceptance, support and joy. As a result you may forget that you made the connection in order to channel information verbally to assist you. From the guide's perspective life is very easy, and it can be difficult to understand that when you are back as your personality self you will be disappointed that you didn't channel verbally.

When we teach channelling we often have one or two people in the group just sitting happily with their guide, and when we connect with them at an energy level we find that they are drifting around in an expanded state of consciousness. At this point we will talk to both channel and guide to remind them that the channel will be sad if no information is brought back to the earth plane.

When you are in that very high space everything seems perfectly obvious. When you are asked a question the answer comes immediately, and it is difficult to understand why anyone would ask something so simple. But when you are back as your personality self the answer does not seem so obvious.

Learning to choose to bring back information is one of the skills of channelling. By doing this you are grounding in your guide's wisdom to the earth plane and to ordinary everyday reality. When you are in the space of your guide you may not want to be bothered to do so, but when you return you will be very pleased that you did.

Channel the answers even when they are obvious

Following from the previous point, people often think that since the answers to questions are so obvious when they are in contact with their guide, they must be answering those questions themselves. This can lead to a lot of doubts. Is it really me? Is it the guide? How can I be sure I am channelling? The best way to be sure you are channelling is to do it. Bring the answers back, note them down or tape them, and then put them away for a few days or weeks or even months. When you look over them later you will be astonished at the depth of the answers you receive, and this will be your confirmation that you really are channelling.

Not everyone hears voices

One common misconception is that channels hear a clear voice in their mind and all they do is to repeat the words they are hearing. This might be your experience of channelling, but the connection is not like this for most people. At the beginning a lot of trust is involved – you just have to let the answers to questions come, and often when you begin a sentence you won't have any idea how you are going to end it. Keep remembering it is not you doing this. Let go of worrying about what the guide will say, and keep out of the way. Your guide will then find it easy to connect with you and to send to your mind the impulses of energy that come out as you channelling in words.

OPENING TO CHANNEL

When we teach a class, I gather all the humans together in a room whilst Ortan gathers all their guides together in one energy location in the higher realms. When the human participants are ready to open to channel they are directed to the place where the guides are waiting for them. The guides can see them reaching up to the higher realms and they in turn are reaching down towards them; their reaching is like a sort of yearning. The human participants reach this energy location by rising up through the planes and dimensions until they reach an energy gateway. By choosing to pass through this gateway they enter into the realms of light. Ortan and the guides will then come forward. At this point, all each human participant has to do is to open his/her heart and ask for his/her guide to come.

Remember, high-level guides will only come to you when specifically asked to do so. Later on in the relationship you can agree how and when you will connect, but at the start high-level guides are especially careful not to intrude on your energetic space. These guides have an extremely strong sense of the integrity of your being. A feeling of unconditional love and respect is the key to knowing that your guide is a high-level one.

Choosing when to connect with your guide

All you have to do is ask your guide to come and assist you, and they will. You may find that you are very conscious of your guide at the beginning. Some people prefer to have distinct times when they connect with their guides. If this is something you would like, discuss it with your guide, explaining that you like a structured relationship.

Connect with the highest possible guide

When the human participants ask their guides to come to them, they do so instantly. At this point it is important to check the energy of the guide. Ortan always directs students to ask two questions of the guide. Firstly, 'Are you from the light?' If the response is not yes, the entity must be firmly requested to leave forthwith. Secondly, ask, 'Are you the highest-level guide that I can channel at this time?' Again, if the guide says no, request them to leave immediately and ask for the highest-level guide to come to you.

There will be no problem. It is a law of this universe that you have only to ask clearly for the entity to leave and it must obey. If you follow a particular religion you may care to ask the entity, 'Do you serve God [or Allah or the Divine]?' All God's names work equally well for this purpose, because energetically the concept of God is the same whatever he or she is actually called. If you are working at home from this book, make sure that you perform this very important step.

Why should you ask to connect with the highest possible guide? By doing so you choose your highest possible path of growth and you align with your highest purpose. As a result you will be able to experience your highest path and a sense of acceleration on your spiritual path. Only by channelling the highest possible guide do you really stretch yourself (for a channelling on this subject see p.131).

MEDITATION: TO CONNECT WITH YOUR GUIDE

The 'third eye' mentioned in this meditation is a chakra (see Chapter 8) in the centre of your forehead. Known also as the ajna centre, it is where your psychic abilities can be awakened.

Begin by finding a comfortable position, letting your body become very relaxed and comfortable and your mind clear and focused.

Spend a few minutes visualizing a wonderful bubble of light forming all around you, and reach up to your soul and ask it to fill this bubble with its light. Try to visualize the light of your soul shining down on you, filling you up with light, and this light also filling the bubble around you with your soul's light. Ask your soul to protect you. Use the process to expand your aura now in readiness to accommodate all the energy that your guide will be holding.

Let yourself choose to make this easy, to make this joyous and to make this sacred. Once again, imagine that you are lifting up, higher and higher, rising up through the clouds, your energy clearing as you lift and you feel the light shining down upon you, clearing your energy, lifting your vibration. Rising up, very safe in your bubble of light. Imagine that your mind is very focused, very clear, very alert and very open. You are rising up higher and higher until you sense that you are reaching a higher plane of reality, you are reaching the realms of the guides. Imagine that there is a gateway between the two realms – you might imagine it as an energy portal. Go very quiet within and decide that you are going to go through this portal. On the other side of the portal take a few moments to adjust to the higher light that is surrounding you.

Now begin to call your guide to come to you. Imagine you are sending lines of radiant light out from your heart to your guide's heart, and with your inner voice call out to that guide to come to you. (Don't worry at this stage if you cannot see the guide in your meditation. Just trust the process and keep going.)

Let your guide come close to you now and ask with your inner voice: 'Are you from the light? Do you have my growth and my spiritual evolution as your priority in our work together. Are you the highest guide I can work with at this time?' If you feel comfortable, and if your guide has answered in the affirmative, continue. If not, go back and call another guide to you. If you have a sense that a guide is present and this is the one that you are to work with, greet this guide warmly, letting your heart energy meld with your guide's heart energy and feel the joy of union. What does your guide look like with your inner vision? Your guide may simply appear as a glow of shimmering light or just an inner feeling, a sense of comfort or just knowingness. Ask your guide now to intensify this feeling so that you will be able to recognize and know when your guide is with you.

Now ask your guide to assist you now in opening your energy, in adjusting your energy, and imagine that the area at the back of your head and neck is open to the light of your guide. Tell your guide that you are now ready for the channelling activation, and visualize the light of your guide shining into the back of your head and neck and into your heart centre. Imagine the light of your guide activating your third eye in the centre of your forehead, opening you up to higher love and to higher wisdom. Ask your guide to continue to strengthen the connection between you. You may feel the connection stabilizing and deepening as you go on. Stay here in this space with your guide as long as you want, letting the connection between you develop and deepen.

Now slowly begin to come back to the room, thanking your guide for all the love and assistance you have been given. Let the bubble of light around you dissolve, and come all the way back.

Once you have connected with a guide who is from the light and is the highest possible guide for you, it is safe to proceed. When you first open to channel, you and the guide are learning how to make a clear, steady, easy connection between you. Remember that this is a two-way learning process – your guide, too, is learning how to connect. Many guides have not been channelled before and have to learn how it is done. So bear in mind that you need to be patient, loving and open towards both your guide and yourself. Give yourselves the time and space to get acquainted.

As the guide moves into your energy you will need to increase the size of your aura (see p.37). As the guide comes in, let your aura expand to accommodate the increase in energy.

Your guide vibrates at a higher, finer frequency than you do. Much of the process of getting to know your guide is about tuning yourself into the frequency of light that is the energy signature of your guide.

THE LIGHT ACTIVATION

Your guide will use a light activation process to trigger your ability to channel. First of all, a ray of light is beamed to an area known as the medulla centre at the base of the skull where your head and neck join. If you move your head very slightly you will be able to bring your awareness to this centre. The ray of light moves down from the back of the head through the body to the heart centre, which is located in the centre of the chest.

The guide then beams a ray of vivid blue or indigo light to activate the third eye in the centre of the forehead. This light opens you to higher love and wisdom and expands your intuitive ability to tune into higher thoughts and your own inner knowingness. This activation may be felt as anything from a slight tingling or even a tickling feeling right through to a very strong physical sensation like an ache or a pulsing or throbbing in the area of the third eye or the physical eyes. Some people experience a slight dizziness or disorientation. The physical sensations soon pass and are not usually uncomfortable – indeed they can be comforting since you know that something is happening.

It is through the activation process that the guide can assist you in increasing your vibration, whilst stepping down their own vibration. This change in vibration is the reason why, when you first connect, you may feel very emotional or just odd. If the guide has not stepped down their vibration sufficiently, you may have problems in tracking the information as it comes through. Commonly, the information comes through so quickly that you are overwhelmed – it can feel as if you are getting nothing because you cannot grasp the information. It is useful to ask your guide to spend some time adjusting their vibration to yours – it is practically impossible to spend too long on this stage.

THE EXPERIENCE OF OPENING

I asked some of my past students what it had been like when they first channelled their guides. Here are some of their responses:

> Before we arrived we felt very excited, yet very nervous – we likened it to going to the dentist. ... On the way home from the channelling weekend we were on a complete high. The car seemed to be flying along and we sang songs all the way home

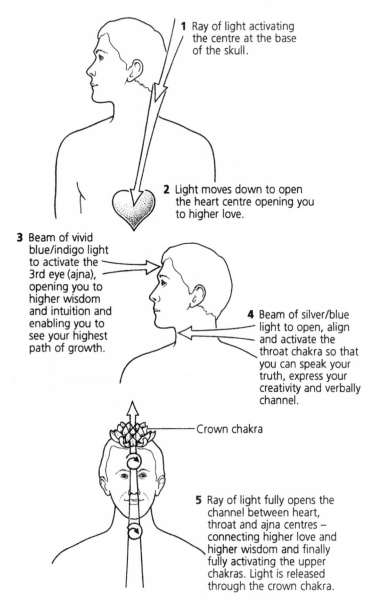

1 Ray of light activating the centre at the base of the skull.

2 Light moves down to open the heart centre opening you to higher love.

3 Beam of vivid blue/indigo light to activate the 3rd eye (ajna), opening you to higher wisdom and intuition and enabling you to see your highest path of growth.

4 Beam of silver/blue light to open, align and activate the throat chakra so that you can speak your truth, express your creativity and verbally channel.

Crown chakra

5 Ray of light fully opens the channel between heart, throat and ajna centres – connecting higher love and higher wisdom and finally fully activating the upper chakras. Light is released through the crown chakra.

The channelling activation

with the music blaring out, like a couple of teenagers! It was a wonderful experience.

The atmosphere in the room on the first morning was amazing. It was also very emotional – the strength of the love that is there touches you very deeply. I felt lots of tingling and energy around my throat, and as soon as I opened my mouth words just came.

It was scary at first, not fully knowing what to expect. Then it became an exhilarating feeling, knowing and finally realizing that there was more than just our physical bodies.

HOW GUIDES COMMUNICATE WITH YOU

Your guide makes the connection with you at a higher level, the soul level. The energy is then transmitted down to you at the personality level. The energy transmissions enter one of the many areas of the brain that lie dormant, and you then find the words to match the transmissions. For a channelling on this topic see p.132.

Physical signals

Many people say they experience a physical sensation when channelling. For example, one student told me, 'I notice a strong feeling like a heaviness between the eye and the nose on the left side of my face.' Another feels a sort of tickling at the top of the head. When I begin to channel Ortan there is a slight movement of my body, and I feel very expanded and extremely peaceful. These feelings are very common and also very pleasant.

It can be useful to ask the guide to strengthen these physical sensations so you know if your guide wants to communicate something to you. It is also very confirming to have these strong signals. A recent student told me that he had asked his guide to twitch his ear when he was present, now his guide will always give him this sensation when present.

Various means of transmitting information

Information can be conveyed in a number of ways. For instance, sometimes the guides arrange for you to acquire knowledge through reading, or talking to others, on the earth plane. Guides will also bring to the surface knowledge that was lying hidden in your subconscious – in other words, things you knew already but were not necessarily aware that you knew. For a channelling on this see p.131.

Assistance from other guides

During readings I have sometimes found that Ortan has suddenly gone away for a few seconds. When his energy returns I have a strong sense of another presence with him – he has gone off to find another guide to help answer the question. Very exceptionally he has gone and made a connection with a person who has died; this has happened when the person really needed to contact the person having the reading. It is not I who make the connection, but Ortan, so he relays the message to me.

It is possible that you have worked with your guide before

Ortan and I have worked together before in past lives (see Chapter 8). We have made an arrangement that, although he connects with our students, he will not be channelled by anyone else in my present lifetime (for a channelling on this see p.133).

Asking for your guide's assistance and wisdom

When you begin you will probably have masses of questions that you would like to channel on. The questions below are the sort that many guides are happy to answer, and may be helpful to you. You could use these questions when you have a friend with you to put the questions on your behalf. If you are on your own you could tape the questions. In either case you will channel the answers.

1. Can you tell the channel what it was that drew you to work with him/her?

2. Have you ever been incarnated? If so, when and where?

3. Can you tell us something about the changes for humanity that are happening now?

4. Is there anything that the channel could do to prepare for these changes?

5. Can you give the channel some advice about how to maintain total, radiant, good health in the physical body?

6. Please will you give the channel some ideas about how to be totally fulfilled and happy in this lifetime?

7. Can you tell the channel about what it was that drew you to work with him/her?

8. Can you give the channel some ideas about how to be more abundant in his/her life at this time?

9. What spiritual practice/s would assist the channel at this time?

10. What is the channel learning in his/her relationship with ——?

11. What is the most important life lesson that the channel is learning at this time?

12. How can the channel bring more joy into his/her life?

13. Is there anything else that you would like to tell the channel? [It is good to finish a session with this type of question each time.]

BEING WITH A GUIDE IN A READING

Although it is rather long, I have included some of this reading, with a client whom I have called Jane, to give you a flavour of what it is like to be with a guide for this purpose. The words are a pale reflection of the energy that accompanies them, especially the feeling of unlimited and unconditional love. Notice that the guides use language slightly differently from the way we do. I call this 'guidespeak' – the phraseology is unconventional, particularly the use of 'dear one'. See Chapter 10 for further channelled material.

The Bodhisattva vow referred to is taken in the Buddhist religion. Those who take it vow to stay on the earth plane, being reborn over and over until everyone is enlightened.

GUIDE:　*Greetings, I am Ortan. I greet you, dear one, with much joy and much light from our realms to your realms. Begin to compose the physical body as we begin to connect at an energetic level, for in some senses the dense matter of the physical body can be something of an encumbrance to you as we communicate in these realms and at these levels, so to speak. And if we can find a tuning between us the information will then move directly from my heart and my energy to your heart and your energy, even though as you understand my heart is not physical. But the heart is always a presence within the energy, and we notice that you are taking a great interest in the affairs of the heart, so to speak, and it is when one such as you starts to reach up and to ask these conscious questions that you will open yourself to the possibility of broader and richer energetic experiences.*

But it is a reaching that must be done by the human person and cannot be done from us to you, for, as we have often explained, it is a law of the universe that you must ask. And a great deal of this ability to open the heart lies in the ability to make a full and conscious connection with the soul, for, as you will understand, at a soul level all is love. There is nothing else that is more important in the frequencies of light than the concept of frequency and the vibration of love, for in the living light which is the substance and body of the divine creator this frequency of love is the most preponderant. You could say it is the one which contains many other frequencies, and because of this it is one of the dominant frequencies of the universe, for there are many sub-frequencies which lie within it.

And we have explained to the channel in the past that there are different types of love, and you are aware of divisions, and in your earthly manifestations there are many kinds of love. But the love that will take you to the soul planes and connect you fully to the soul is the resonance of compassion. This is the key frequency of love. It contains many other frequencies, and when it manifests upon the earth plane it manifests in many forms. But in these forms there are always commonalities, and these commonalities will tell you that it is compassion that is present. There will never be a mistaking of compassion, for it is such a strong and dominant vibrational frequency.

Connecting into the frequencies of compassion and opening the heart to the extent that you wish to do can be achieved upon the earth plane by taking the Bodhisattva vow. But you must understand that in taking vows you will bind yourself karmically for all time, and we do not advise that vows are taken without very, very much consideration of the meaning of such a binding upon the karma for so much possible time. Indeed, for an infinity of time, upon the earth plane the Bodhisattva vow has been of great importance and many of the greatest teachers have taken it. But it is one that you must take after several months or years of contemplation and understanding the true meaning of what this could do and how this could change you. And it may be that your personality, your lower self, will not be ready for such commitment. But the path that leads to the vow is one that is quite well understood among humans, and upon the earth plane there is instruction.

The easiest way for you to do this is to consciously reach up to the soul. It is the soul level that will open the heart fully, for when you exist fully as your soul your heart will be completely open, your experience will be unbounded expansiveness, an understanding of the true, unbounded and limitless abundance of all that there is. And this abundance especially concerns the frequencies of love, for there is no limit to love – it is all about you. By tuning into this abundance of frequencies, this abundance of love, of course you will tune into an abundance of all else your heart desires. But the interesting paradox of human growth is that when humans open to true compassion they are no longer interested in all the abundance of manifestation in quite the same way. They find the simple sight of a butterfly, the ripple of water, the rising of the sun, to be more exquisite than any beautiful antique or lovely painting. Although these two will still be appreciated as the beautiful products of skilled hands, yet it is the natural and divine-sourced manifestations which will give the most pleasure. And there will not be much pleasure in watching the accumulation of the money within the bank account, for this trivial manifestation is not one that introduces much joy. It may bring happiness, but this is a different frequency. But it is not an untrammelled frequency of joy, which is part of the compassion range.

JANE: When I experienced the state of having the heart open it was far more enjoyable than anything I could have imagined to do with achieving any other desire. When you say 'Bodhisattva vow' is that state what you mean?

GUIDE: *The Bodhisattva vow is the vow of service, dear one, of achieving enlightenment but not choosing ascension, and this is an interesting balance. Those who choose the Bodhisattva path are those who will be admitted into the heart of God, but they choose to stay without until all can enter the heart of God. It is an especially special path of service. By choosing such an open-hearted path of service one's process of understanding the heart of God is opened more easily, but it has to be 100 per cent dedication to service and it is not for all to take. It is the path that is chosen by the great teachers, by the great healers, by the great servers of mankind. All the angels have taken similar vows – although on their plane they are not manifest, of course – but all the angels have chosen such an existence. They will not be enfolded once more to the heart of God until all beings, all entities reach that heart. And it is this service of others, this joy in opening your heart to humanity, that is an important key in achieving the pure joy of compassion.*

Compassion, the opening of the heart, is not a selfish pursuit, for all personal development, all spiritual growth is carried out on a path of service. Those who are not on the path of service show little interest in spiritual growth, dear one, for they cannot see the point of it. And they will even tell you that it is a selfish pursuit, which is an interesting view. For by increasing your own frequency you make it easier for those behind you to follow you, and you are able to extend your heart and your hand to those who are willing to grow. And by your example and your beautiful, true, open heart you will lead them through the gateway to the heart of God, which is always open, always available. Regrettably, few yet are awakening to the true possibility of such an experience, but your experience at the weekend, dear one, was the beginnings of what it is like to truly have the heart of your soul upon the earth plane.

There is another thing we would say to you about this experience, and this is that it is important that you do not grasp after experiences of this type. They will arise, but they cannot be grasped after. If you spend time trying to be in that experience you will close yourself off from other avenues, and you will indeed close yourself off from that experience. For it is only when you completely give up grasping for experience that experience can arise. It is the pure unbounded ground of consciousness that you are starting to contact here, the clear blue sky of awareness.

JANE: So instead of trying to re-create that experience, what would you suggest as a means to open the heart more? Not to re-create it, but to actually create it?

GUIDE: *Correct. The way to open the heart now is to first of all release yourself from any expectations. Humans are truly bounded many times by expectations of how it should be, how it ought to be, how it must be, where they want to go, how they must go there and all of these things. So when we talk of letting go of expectation we mean simply following simple spiritual practice, with no thought other than joy at the practice. To do this you must follow your heart.*

Now, this sounds like a paradox. But what we mean by this is that you must look about you and find the frequencies within activities that reflect the frequencies of an open heart. And it is a key to know that joy is one of these frequencies. Therefore your spiritual practice is the practice that will bring you joy. However, although at first your heart may leap with joy and you may find the practice to be fun, to be enjoyable, there will be times when the practice will become onerous. These are the times when discipline and integrity become important. Do you understand this?

So the open-hearted meditations are always centred around working to love all humanity, first of all practising the loving kindness, the metta meditation of the Buddhists. It is a very tried and tested technique to opening the heart. It is easy, it is simple, it is pure — but regularly practised it is very effective. Opening the heart involves opening the heart to loving the self and to loving all who come to you for assistance without depleting the self, finding the lines, the boundaries, the places to be where you are truly yourself, at one with your own energy. And yet you are centring your awareness within the heart centre, as if you could move your awareness from wherever it is at the moment into the heart, as if you looked out from that jewel in the heart. Do you understand that? If you looked out from your heart, what would you see?

JANE: Myself, I think.

GUIDE: *You would indeed see yourself, and you would see the world from the perspective of loving light. One of the keys to opening the heart is to live within the living light of God, and looking out from your heart you would begin to see the light emanating from source. And this would indeed change your experience. Do you understand this?*

It is a practice. Play with it, move your awareness to the heart and look out, play, notice, observe. Another practice that is most important is observation and mindfulness of the moment – no grasping and no expectation, staying entirely in this moment, enjoying all that is present at this time, not looking forwards nor looking back, not asking, not accepting, simply being. For it is very difficult for humans working with matter to be in a state of pure unbounded awareness, but this too is one of the answers to opening the heart.

JANE: I usually think there is something more that I should be doing.

GUIDE: *When you get to that stage you must look deep within the experience. You do not float or drift, you become more focused. And as you focus you move the light more deeply into your experience. As you do this you start to uncover other states of awareness. It is one of the spiritual traps of the path to be in the joy of apparent nirvana, but there is far, far more beyond this particular state. And this is only a state of beginners who arrive at the state and think that they are there. Regrettably, nothing further will happen. It is important at that stage to then look more deeply into the heart, to really start to delve deeply into your experience, and to call upon the divine source for assistance in going more deeply.*

JANE: Is it possible for me to reach a stage when I do love everybody?

GUIDE: *Most certainly. It is rare, but it is most possible.*

JANE: Can you suggest anything to practise?

GUIDE: *Certain forms of yoga are beneficial in opening all the energy centres. The key to it is this: the physical body must be 100 per cent healthy, all the meridians balanced and flowing, all the simple systems of the body, the chakras, the meridians, the chi must all flow, be aligned and in balance. The higher frequencies of energy, the light body frequencies also need to be aligned so that the physical body is in perfect balance. Because you are born into a world of matter, to anchor in the perfect experience depends upon a total flow within the physical body, if you can achieve it.*

This is not to say that those who are physically disabled are unable to have these states. What it means is that they must find the perfect flow within the structure that they have been given to work with – perfect flow and a full connection with the soul. For as you bring the soul down through the antakarana then you will be able to live with a totally open heart, looking out from the heart as your soul. It is this key that will really change this experience.

6

AFTER CHANNELLING: THE WAY AHEAD

Channels reaching to these realms are opening doorways all over the planet.

ORTAN

Well, you've done it – you've channelled a guide! How are you feeling? At this point it is quite normal for doubts to arise. People often say, 'Is this real? . . . I'm not sure if I was really channelling. . . . I'm making it all up – it's really only me.'

DOUBTS

All these doubts are part of the channelling process. When you are in the channelling space with your guide, the answers to questions look so obvious that it can be difficult to believe that it is not you just pretending to channel. But remember that doubts are your friends – they show that you have a questioning mind. You are not just going to accept everything that you are told – you ask questions, you wonder, you test. Your guide will not be offended that you are doing this; quite the reverse. Ortan always stresses that those who doubt often make the very best channels. It is a sign of intelligence and, above all, of an ability to discern what is high and good and what is not.

It is also helpful when working with doubts to think about how the guide accesses your brain and all the things you know. Guides are always very efficient in the way they bring information to you, so if the answer to a question can be found easily on the earth plane they may just tell you to read a book, attend a class or talk to a certain person. But they may not do so directly. For instance, if you have read a particular book and you suddenly remember a passage from it when you ask the guide a question, why do you think that happened? The answer is that it is a form of matching – the guide's transmissions are matching that information in your brain, and you then access that information as the correct answer to the question you have asked. Similarly, people often say that their guide's answers utilize their own past experiences and learning. Of course they do! The answer is already there and the guide is merely pointing it out to you.

Many channels look for confirmation that the information they have received is indeed from a guide and not just from their own mind, but it can be very difficult to provide confirmation easily and in a way that a doubting person will accept if they don't want to. However, confirmation will be given. Stay open, and don't expect it necessarily to come in the way that you expect.

Over the years that I have worked with Ortan he has often given me confirmation, which I have greatly appreciated. Ask your guide to help – guides are very clever at providing confirmation in a way that is special to you and that you will understand.

Sometimes, during a reading, Ortan will use a term that is known only to the person asking the questions. For instance, when one woman came for a reading he referred to her friend as 'that lovely lady', which is her private pet name. Often he pinpoints a physical symptom that the client is currently experiencing. Another woman had a problem with her knee which she had not mentioned and which was not obvious in any way, yet Ortan spoke about it. He frequently does this kind of thing at the beginning of a reading, presumably to reassure people and put them at ease.

ASSESSING CHANNELS

You may also be interested in assessing whether someone else is really channelling. Many of our students have asked how they can tell if someone else is channelling a high-level guide, or if the things that they themselves are being told through their own thoughts are actually from a high-level guide. Here are some ways to do so.

High-level guides don't flatter you

True high-level guides don't flatter you; astral entities do. Astral-level entities (see p.116) will build up your ego whenever they can. High-level guides will certainly congratulate you on your successes, but that is all.

David Furlong, a very respected healer and teacher, made some interesting comments in a piece published in the spring 1998 issue of *Kindred Spirit* magazine:

> Another subtle hook is that of ego inflation. We all like to think that we are serving a 'higher cause'. Over the years I have heard many exaggerated claims made by individuals in certain groups that they were very special, an elite organization, working for the salvation of the planet in a way that only they could fulfil. Let me emphatically state that anyone who has the love of God in their heart that is expressed openly and freely is a special person with an important mission to fulfil. . . . Take care not to be taken in by such enticements, for curbing the ego is one of the first steps of spiritual development.
>
> Into this category I would also place those teachers, whether incarnate or in channelled form, who claim that they were a great named person from the past ('In my former life as King Solomon . . .'). Underlying all these statements is fear, for if the teaching or message is right it will stand on its own merit. It should not require the prop of some past association, however seemingly significant. As the Buddha stated, we should accept things, not just because they come from a sage or a famous person, but when they accord with what lies within our own heart.

High-level guides don't try to control you

High-level guides make suggestions about things you might do and offer alternatives, maybe even giving a perspective you hadn't thought of. But they don't order you to do things or seek to control you. Guides always let you know that it is a free-will universe and all the choices are ultimately your own.

High-level guides encourage you to do what strengthens and empowers you

Guides try to encourage you to be independent, not dependent. Above all else they are oriented to your growth. Sometimes you need to make mistakes in order to learn, but guides will not criticize you for that. Instead, they will encourage you to learn the lesson and move on.

High-level guides don't try to make you feel guilty

Guides don't try to make you feel bad about your actions; instead they will point out in the kindest and gentlest possible way where you could do better. They certainly will not take a position of suggesting that they are 'better' than you or more important than you. They don't claim to be the ultimate authority – they know that they are not.

High-level guides are loving and kind and don't try to frighten you

Be concerned if a guide's messages appear frightening. Fear is a tool of lower-level entities and not of high-level guides.

Practise Makes Perfect

Once you have made a connection with your guide, the most important thing is to practise channelling. Whether you are channelling verbally, or writing or healing or painting, does not matter – the connection will be strengthened and enhanced by being made repeatedly.

The more you channel, the easier it becomes. It is rather like learning a new form of exercise: the more you use the muscles, the stronger and better developed they become and the easier it is to do the exercises.

When people ask how often they should channel, I always tell them to do so as frequently as they can remember to do it. Talk to your guide in your mind and ask for help in your life. Your guide is always there, waiting to assist you and to make the connection with you.

GROUNDING

Sometimes when you come back from meditation or from the channelling space you might feel less able than usual to handle the physical world. For example, you may be slightly more clumsy than normal or unable to concentrate. If this is the case, you probably need to pay more attention to grounding.

Grounding centres and realigns your energy, connecting you back to base. Here are a number of techniques to choose from.

1. Have a cup of tea or other hot drink and a biscuit or something sweet. Hot food is an excellent way to ground yourself.

2. Take some form of physical exercise, like walking or jogging.

3. Hug a tree or connect with nature in your own way. Try placing the palms of your hands flat on the ground and feeling your energy merging with that of the earth.

4. Visualize a ray of light going down into the earth from your base chakra at the bottom of your spine. Feel the connection being made. It can help if you visualize a crystal in the centre of the planet into which you are connecting. Feel the light going into the crystal and back out again to you.

5. Hold a grounding crystal, like obsidian or haematite, in your hand and ask for assistance from it.

6. If you have your hands palm upwards during meditation, reverse the position so that your palms are resting on your legs, facing down. When the palms are facing upwards you are more open to energy; when they face down you are closing down your receptiveness and thus orienting yourself back to the everyday world. Try different ways of positioning your hands – it makes a difference.

7. Stamp your feet and walk about the room, breathing deeply.

MAKING CHANGES IN YOUR LIFE

As you develop as a channel it brings changes to you and to your life. As Ortan has pointed out, this is not always a welcome development. Channelling opens you up to compassion and love and, of course, to changes at the most basic level. If you decide to become a channel as part of your spiritual growth, you need to be ready to make changes at all levels in your life.

These changes may happen in spite of yourself. When you channel you become open to a much wider view: your guide's energy connection will expand your ability to be conscious at an increasing number of levels – physical, mental, emotional and spiritual. Like all energy work, channelling is a form of surrender to growth. Some people find this too much and close down again. The changes needed in their lives are too challenging or too frightening, or they feel that they aren't ready.

Channelling can be part of your spiritual growth if you choose it. One student wrote this to let me know about the changes that were taking place for him after taking an Opening to Channel class: 'The course I took with you almost a year ago has certainly changed my life, and my path of growth is racing towards me at full speed and taking no prisoners. Various events have led to me losing my job and I've been plunged into a survival crisis, which is quite scary but somehow feels right for me. The same compelling forces that brought me to your Opening to Channel class are busy rearranging a new life for me, and where there was once restriction there are now unlimited opportunities.'

This is a very typical experience when you decide to channel: at one level there is fear and at another tremendous excitement at taking this opportunity for growth. By connecting with the higher realms consciously you move towards tremendous changes, especially in the area of the ego. Our egos try so hard to be in control, but channelling well requires complete abnegation of the ego. This is why very egotistical people don't make good channels – they just can't stay out of the way enough to be a clear channel.

But when you channel you are able to find out who you really are and why you are here – you constantly discover more about your higher purpose, your soul and your own unique path of growth. As you channel and open to love and light in your life, you create a wonderful flowing energy within you. This flow is the natural state for all healthy beings.

It is this inflow of energy and light that brings about the changes you encounter when you become a channel. You can stop the process by closing down – by just stopping all contact with guides and their energy – and gradually things will go back to the way they were. It is difficult to see why you would want to do that, though, once you have experienced the way in which higher beings operate and once you realize that you too have the possibility of being, like them, clear and happy, kind and fulfilled.

7

CHANNELLING FOR OTHERS

By your allowing us to assist you, you allow us to grow, for our commitment, our mission, is a mission of service until all of you who are upon the earth plane have reached your fullest potential, until all of you have reached fulfilment and enlightenment.

ORTAN

CHOOSING YOUR CHANNELLING PARTNER

When you are ready to do a reading for another person, here are a few suggestions. The easiest way is to begin by channelling for a trusted and sympathetic friend, perhaps for just fifteen or twenty minutes at a time. Choose friends who are supportive; even better, if at all possible, choose friends who also channel, then you can take it in turns to channel for each other.

Firstly, only channel for someone else when you feel absolutely ready – you don't need to prove anything to anyone. Don't do a reading if you aren't feeling well or if you're tired or under the influence of drugs or alcohol.

PREPARATION

When someone books a reading with Ortan, we send them a sheet outlining what to expect and how to prepare. This is rather formal if you are just doing a reading for a friend, but it helps if you explain to your friend that preparation is an integral part of the process of having a reading. Over and over again clients remark that having to sit down and figure out the questions has been a very useful exercise in itself, helping them to see what their priorities are and the areas where they really need help.

A copy of the sheet we send out is shown on p.89. We also include our name, address and telephone number, of course, together with directions for finding the School of the Living Light, and we quote the current fee for a reading. Many of our students have copied this sheet in their own literature, maybe editing some of it to suit their own needs, and you may like to do the same. You will find that people get a lot more out of the reading if they have spent this time in preparation.

Before my client arrives I spend a few minutes in meditation and make a connection with them at a soul level. I hold them in my heart and I call in my guide to assist me. After this I check that the room where we will be working is well aired and at a comfortable temperature. A box of tissues is useful as readings can often make people shed a few tears.

I have two tape recorders, one equipped with a small clip-on microphone through which I record the readings, the other for playing gentle music which helps me to concentrate and sets the scene for your client. It is also pleasant to have some fresh flowers in the room. Crystals can help to absorb negative energy, for which purpose I always have a couple of amethyst clusters in the room. Be sure to cleanse your crystals frequently.

MAKING YOUR CLIENT FEEL AT HOME

When your client arrives make sure they are comfortable, show them where the bathroom is and offer water or tea or whatever is appropriate. Clients are often very nervous when they come for a reading, so they need a few minutes to settle down before starting. Many clients expect a reading to be 'spooky' in some way, and are immensely reassured when they see that I look just like everybody else and that the surroundings are also quite normal. I

Making the Most of a Channelled Reading with Ortan

Ortan is a Being of Light who exists in the Higher Realms. He has not been incarnate on the earth plane as far as we know. He is a very loving being who serves those who wish to follow a spiritual path in this lifetime. He is a teacher guide.

If you are at a change point in your life, or if you feel that you are unsure about how to deal with problems in your life, then a reading with Ortan may be beneficial for you. He will not necessarily give cut and dried answers, but he will offer ideas for resolution of problems, or perhaps he will give a new perspective on them. Ortan is especially interested in giving spiritual guidance to genuine seekers of knowledge and often gives exercises and practices which you can follow to enhance your own spiritual development.

Lita does not channel people who have passed on, only guides. Ortan does not answer questions about the future, he stresses that he is not a fortune teller and that this is a Free Will universe, there are only probable futures and there are no fixed outcomes. He will, however, explore possible courses of action with you, but he never tells people what to do. Guides never take away your freedom of action and they stress that they never take away your lessons in this lifetime.

Lita and Ortan also offer Past Life Readings during which you and Ortan can explore the influence of past life experiences and lessons on this life.

Allow about an hour for your visit. If you wish to tape the reading then please bring a blank cassette with you. You should be aware that tape recordings of readings are not always successful, although we do seem to be getting better at it! It can also be beneficial to spend some time before the reading considering what you would like to discuss with Ortan, perhaps making a list of topics you want to cover, then you will not forget anything when you get here.

begin by talking for a few minutes, first asking whether they have had a channelled reading before. They usually say no. Even if they say yes I explain that I am going to tell them about having a reading with Ortan so that they are quite clear about what is going to happen.

I say something along the following lines:

'I am Lita and I will be channelling my guide Ortan for you in a few minutes' time. When I am channelling I will be sitting in this chair with my eyes closed, in a state of light meditation. At the same time I will be playing some music on this tape machine and recording your reading on that tape machine. When my guide comes he will say, "Greetings, I am Ortan." When the reading is finished my guide will conclude by saying ". . . and I bid you my loving farewell for now." Then you know that he has gone.

'In between these two things readings are very individual and it is difficult to say exactly what will happen. You should be aware that, although the guide is talking to you, at the same time he is making an energy connection with you. This can lead to some people feeling a bit spacey or emotional or just a bit "different". But there's nothing to worry about – the guide will not do anything without your permission. So if, for example, the guide thinks that some healing work will be beneficial to you, he will first ask if you feel comfortable with that. If you don't, he won't offer the healing. The energy connection is the way that guides naturally connect – they are energy beings and they see us as energy beings too. So when I am channelling I "see" you through my guide's "eyes" rather than as I see you now through my own physical eyes.

'When I come back from the reading I may be a little disoriented for a few seconds, so just give me a moment to come back fully. I will remember what happened during the reading when I come back, but this memory will swiftly fade so that by tomorrow I won't remember anything about the reading.

'The guide will talk to you just as I am talking to you now. He may well put questions to you or ask for clarification. Just talk to him naturally as you do to me. Don't worry – you can't offend a guide or ask anything in the wrong way.

'Are there any questions you would like to ask before we begin?'

GIVING THE READING

Many people are concerned that their questions may not be the 'right sort', and it is helpful to reassure them that they can't ask 'wrong' questions! Guides are so skilful at handling questions that they often help the client to focus in on what they really want to know. Clients are also often worried that their questions are not 'deep' enough or 'spiritual' enough. I explain that if something is important to them it is important enough to ask a guide. Guides are in service, Ortan has chosen to be channelled, and he doesn't make value judgements about the questions he is asked.

It can be helpful to explain, though, that if it is not the right time for the client to know the answer to a question then the guide will not give it. It may be, for instance, that the lessons of a particular experience are not yet completed and to point them out is premature. In past life readings Ortan will sometimes quickly pass over certain past lives and explain that there is no value for the client in knowing about them.

When Ortan and I were first working together I thought there would be limits on what topics he would discuss, but I quickly learned that he was interested in all kinds of things. For example, we were invited to teach channelling and carry out some readings in Hong Kong, a place where money and commercial interests are paramount. I had always thought my guide wasn't interested in such issues, but when a high-powered Chinese businessman came along Ortan proceeded to tell him how to run his business and how to organize his staff. I was amazed. The businessman loved it and said afterwards how useful it had been. I realized that I would have to stop telling people that Ortan doesn't know about business. He looks at it not from the management perspective but from an energy point of view: he just looked at the energy of what the client was bringing before him and talked to him about it.

Sometimes, when people come for readings, they'll ask a question and I know that Ortan has gone. He has gone off somewhere, acquired the information and brought it back for them. This only takes a matter of moments, but can be alarming as you know that the connection between you and the guide has gone into a suspended state. However, guides are not in the habit of leaving you in the lurch, and their temporary absence feels different from the feeling of losing your connection with the guide. When you are losing the connection your mind starts to come in and there is a sense of 'fading', whereas when the guide is going off to obtain information the break is cleaner and you feel as if you are left hanging. It often feels subjectively like a long time, but really it isn't, so stay calm and wait.

The information that proves hardest to allow through is often the most important to channel for your client, so let yourself be stretched and keep your mind out of the way. Remember, one of the biggest mistakes you can make as a channel is to try and edit or decide yourself what should or should not be said to your client. Your guide knows exactly what to do and say, so just keep out of the way.

When you come back into the room after the reading, spend a few minutes discussing what happened with your client. This will help them to integrate the information and allows time for any other questions that they may have once the reading is over.

8

CHANNELLING ON SPECIAL ISSUES

You can heal in the present everything from the past, and indeed you can heal your future too.

ORTAN

PAST LIVES

In this chapter I am going to focus on channelling about certain specific topics, starting with past lives. Each of us is a soul who has chosen to incarnate in a human body. But this is not the first time you have lived in a human body, and it probably won't be the last either. There are several techniques that you can use to find out about past lives, and channelling is only one of them; other techniques include meditation and hypnotic regression. For channellings that talk about past lives see pp.136 and 148.

Ortan and I are often asked to channel for people about their past lives. Channelling in this way is really no different from any other reading you can do. However, there are a few things you need to consider before embarking on this technique.

Don't neglect the present

Sometimes you will not get anything through at all that relates to past lives. If this happens don't worry: your guide will explain to your client what is happening and will also point out that it is clearly something in this life that will help them, not in a past life. At times we conveniently choose to attribute our present-day difficulties to past life karma and unresolved issues, but this can be a way of avoiding facing up to what we really need to work with, perhaps because it is uncomfortable or difficult for us.

It is also important not to over-emphasize the importance of past lives – we are born into this life to learn our lessons in the present. When we take on the physical incarnation the veil of forgetfulness comes down to cloak our memories so that we can be here in the present. Our soul chose this set of circumstances as being the environment that would most facilitate this learning. Therefore past life readings, whilst often deeply revealing, should not be given too frequently, particularly to the same person.

The time must be right

Ortan explains that it is not always the right time for us to remember a past life. Idle curiosity, he adds, is not an especially high motivation, and we will be given past life information as and when it will help us in our growth. This very rarely happens in a reading, because people simply don't come to a reading if it is not their time to have the experience. Nowadays I trust the guides to take care of this for me – if someone books in for a past life reading I know that if they are supposed to be here they'll arrive and if not they won't. Ortan always says that we don't need to worry about these issues as the energy will take care of it for us. Another lesson in trust!

Conducting the channelling

The most effective method for channelling on past lives is to ask your client to focus on a situation in their present life about which they would like some insight – past life readings often throw an immense amount of light on present life problems and experiences. You don't need to know all the ins and outs of the present-day situation; just let your client focus in, and then become very open to what comes through for you. For me the past life readings are intensely visual. It is like watching a film – the picture suddenly comes up and Ortan gives the commentary. Often I have absolutely no idea why we are seeing the scenes until the end of the reading when he pulls it all together. I find these readings extremely interesting, as through them I have learnt a tremendous amount myself. The best piece of advice I can give you is to stay detached and just let it all run on. Often the clients are very moved by the information; just stay in the channelling space and trust your guide.

When you want to channel for yourself just go into a meditative state, focus on your present-day problem and be very open as you connect with your guide. Remember, you won't always get past life information – it will come if it is appropriate.

Relating past and present lives

Often Ortan will talk to people in some detail about their past lives and the impact of these lives on their present lives. One lady who came to us for a reading had had a past life in India. When we first tuned into this life she was a boy of about fourteen, taking a pair of oxen down a dusty road to a waterhole to drink. The boy was a Hindu who had fallen in love with his employer's daughter. But under the caste system he had no hope of any kind of a relationship with her and he kept this love a secret. The reading moved on to the scene of his death in a hut with his sister holding his hand. He was only seventeen and had wasted away after the girl he loved was married to a man who lived far away and he knew he could never even catch a glimpse of her again. The boy died with his secret locked away.

In her present-day life this lady was unable to let go of her emotions and had consented to an arranged marriage. She did not really love her husband, although she felt that he was a good man. She had carried over from her past life her belief that her real feelings could not be expressed or she would be punished. Once she realized where this came from, Ortan was able to take her back in time to heal herself as that young boy, forgiving him and allowing him to release his secret love.

Another lady who came for a reading asked about her relationship with her present-day husband. Ortan told her that she had been in a previous life with her husband in Edwardian times. Her mother had died and she lived with her father and two brothers. She worked in a publishers, and her present-day husband was her boss in that past life. She had been very fiery and feisty and had never married or had children.

Her present-day husband had been very successful. In this present-day life he had decided to be much more laid back about making money. She too in the past life had been quite well off. Her ideas about money had sprung both from her present-day upbringing and from leftover beliefs from that past life, in which she felt she didn't have to take responsibility for financial matters as her father had always done that. In the past life she had found that her boss (present-day husband) was very responsible and she felt safe with him, because she always felt he would take the right decisions. In the present-day life she and her husband had accumulated a very large debt because of these beliefs.

Her relationship with her husband was that of a brother and sister. She had no children and told me later that in this life she was a successful writer who had published three books. It was interesting to see how some of her past life skills had been carried over to this life, and also how the past life information made so much sense to her when she looked at her current relationship with her husband.

PHYSICAL HEALTH AND WELLBEING

Let's look now at another way of focusing your channelling – on health issues, chakras and auras. Working with your guide, you will find with practice that you can assess the state of another person's energy simply by scanning the chakras and the aura. This scanning involves tuning into the energy of the other person whilst you are connected with your guide.

Guides' interest in physical matters

You will first need to check with your own guide that this is an area in which he has an interest. Ortan is passionately concerned about physical health and wellbeing, but my other guide, Shalaya, has no interest in these matters at all. Ortan often shares physicality with me – he likes to go for walks, to do yoga, to dance. Through me he explores how the body operates, how the energies flow and don't flow, and he has come to his own understanding of all this which he now uses to assist other people in readings.

Shalaya, on the other hand, is dismayed by the experience of physicality. When I first channelled Shalaya he transmitted a deep sadness at my being trapped in this dense field of matter. By doing this he liberated my awareness in a new way: I felt a deep understanding that this experience of being in a physical body is a transitory one and does not express anything like the full range of my potential as a being.

At first sight it may seem very strange that a guide who is non-physical should take any interest in physical health. But Ortan has explained this to me, focusing on two main ideas. The first is that some guides, simply because they *are* non-physical, find the whole area of manifesting, of being at this vibration that we resonate at, fascinating precisely because it is a different vibration from their own. The second reason is that guides realize it can be very difficult to focus on spiritual growth, meditation and spiritual exercises if your body is not working well. This does not necessarily mean that you need perfect health to be spiritual – indeed, many spiritual lessons can be learned through being unwell.

The purpose of illness

Interestingly, many mystics and spiritual people have experienced a great deal of illness, often in childhood. At these times they were forced into isolation and contemplation by their physical condition. This was the case for me: much of my childhood was spent in illnesses that kept me in my bed, thinking, reading and communing with the higher realms. Later in my life cancer too brought many lessons.

It is my belief that ill health is another route to spiritual growth. I have met many people who started on their path of spiritual growth and personal development because they were ill. Finding that conventional medicine was unable to help them, they turned to alternative or complementary approaches. On that journey they learned many things, one of which was the importance of taking responsibility for one's own health rather than just handing the problem over to a doctor. Even our language reflects the way we think about health – many people talk about being 'under the doctor'.

A word of caution

One word of caution before you go further – unless you are a qualified doctor you should never attempt to diagnose a person's illness. Always suggest that your client first visits a properly qualified doctor so that they may make informed decisions about the types of treatment they choose. Once they have the diagnosis they may or may not tell you what it is. In a sense that doesn't matter, for you are reading their energy, but don't make any further claims than that.

Subtle anatomy: chakras and auras

Before you begin to work with your guide to view what is called subtle anatomy – chakras and auras – let's start by being clear about what these are. Everybody has seven major chakras in the body, and 122 minor chakras. The major chakras are roughly aligned down the etheric spine, which runs down the etheric body. This 'body' is like a sheath of energy around the physical body and constitutes the first layer of the aura. The minor chakras are found at the joints. The chakras are centres of force and are located throughout the auric layers/bodies. When you are looking at another person's energy fields you may 'see' both major and minor chakras or only the major chakras. Your guide will know what is important for the reading, so just go with it.

Before you begin to read chakras or auras I strongly recommend that you spend some time working with these energy centres yourself. The benefits of doing so are tremendous and will help you enormously with your channelling and spiritual development. When we decide to work with the chakras, we decide to work to discover ourselves at many levels and in new and unfamiliar ways. Meditation is the route to this work – the symbols and information we have about the chakras serve as the basis of visualizations and as a focus for meditation.

Yoga too can be used as a route to awaken the chakras, but mainly as a preparation for the deeper meditative work.

The yoga postures not only give physical strength and flexibility but also have an impact upon the nadis, the channels which circulate the subtle energies. These subtle energies are very responsive to breathing – prana, life force energy, can be directed by controlled breathing exercises or pranayama. The yoga master Iyengar says that through the practice of pranayama kundalini will be awakened. Kundalini refers to the awakening of the energy that is said to lie curled within the base chakra, often represented as a snake or a serpent. When awakened, the energy rises up through the seven major chakras. If you are not ready for this experience it can be very painful and extremely disorienting. For this reason, breathing exercises are not recommended without specific teaching from an experienced teacher.

Chakras

The chakras are like wheels of energy – the word chakra is Sanskrit for wheel or circle. The chakras are always turning, but how fast they turn depends to some extent upon the wellbeing of the individual. The size, shape, amount of movement and intensity of each chakra are all related to the individual's wellbeing and level of personal development. Dowsing can be used to ascertain the current state of the chakras: you hold a pendulum above the relevant chakra and let it begin to swing with the movement of the chakra. Barbara Brennan (see Bibliography) explains this technique well.

Each chakra can be stimulated or quietened through the use of meditation, chanting, yoga, colours, crystals and fragrances. By bringing the chakras into balance and alignment many positive benefits can be achieved. Each chakra enhances certain qualities – physical, mental and spiritual. Keeping the chakras open and balanced ensures a free flow of energy in the body, which will bring positive feelings and good physical health.

As you work with the chakras and the aura you may come to understand that these concepts are crucial. It is energy which determines our level of health – both the energy that we have running through our chakras and aura, and the energies we are exposed to and thus have to transmute. Duane Packer's guide DaBen has some useful words of advice: he always says that there is no such thing as negative energy – just energy that you cannot handle yet. By working with the chakra system you will increase the range of energies that you are able to transmute and reduce the impact that energies that are not compatible with your own will have on you at all levels.

'Seeing' with your guide

When you share sensing with your guide you can develop your ability to perceive. You begin to be able to perceive auras and chakras, even other people's thoughts in some instances. In short, you become a lot more sensitive.

When you view chakras three main things can be 'seen'. You can observe the direction of the spinning or rotation of the chakra, its shape and diameter. When you look at someone in front of you, facing them, the chakras spin clockwise in healthy people who live above the equator. (In people who live below the equator they spin counter-clockwise, according to Rosalyn Bruyere.)

Energy is drawn up into the first chakra and then moves up in a serpentine movement, into the first chakra and out again, up into the second chakra, out of the third chakra, into the fourth

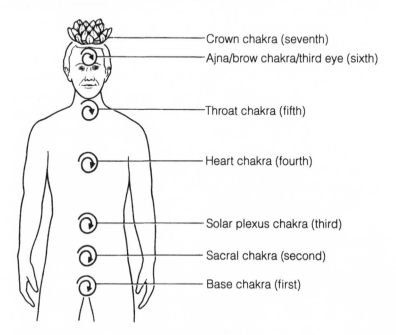

Crown chakra (seventh)

Ajna/brow chakra/third eye (sixth)

Throat chakra (fifth)

Heart chakra (fourth)

Solar plexus chakra (third)

Sacral chakra (second)

Base chakra (first)

The seven major chakras

chakra, out of the fifth chakra, into the sixth chakra and out through the top of the seventh chakra. It is the clockwise spin that draws the energy up to the next chakra. It is useful to remember that the chakras work as a whole system and need to be 'read' together, as they impact on each other all the time.

Each chakra has a polarity, based on whether the energy is moving in or out of it. Ortan often mentions the importance of polarity in our world. The polarities of Yin and Yang, mentioned in the table below, describe energy: Yin is female/passive, Yang male/active. In the chakra system the polarities are as follows:

Chakra	Polarity		
First Chakra	Positive	Energy out	Yang
Second Chakra	Negative	Energy in	Yin
Third Chakra	Positive	Energy out	Yang
Fourth Chakra	Negative	Energy in	Yin
Fifth Chakra	Positive	Energy out	Yang
Sixth Chakra	Negative	Energy in	Yin
Seventh Chakra	Positive	Energy out	Yang

In the table above, negative refers to the flow of energy and does not indicate a negative experience. All these energy fields are electromagnetic in nature: when electrons flow in there is a negative charge, and when they flow out there is a positive charge. Notice also from the table that there is a relationship between the chakras, based on whether they are negative or positive. If you want to manifest changes in your energy you need to work specifically with the positive chakras from which energy flows. If you want to maintain a certain energy set-up you need to work with the negative chakras to keep that set-up. Thus by energizing certain sets of chakras we are able to influence our experience, and of course if you work with other people at an energy level you will be able to influence their experience, too, through working with the chakra system.

When a chakra is round, spinning in a clockwise movement and matches the other chakras in diameter, then it is most probably absolutely fine. However, as you work with other people you

The Seven Chakras and their Correlations

Chakra	Associated Body Parts	Endocrine Glands	Malfunctions at a Physical Level	Colour
First (base)	Spinal column, bones, teeth, nails, legs, feet. Anus, rectum, colon, prostate gland, large intestine. Blood and building of cells	Adrenals	Lack of stamina and physical energy levels low, obesity, constipation, sciatica, degenerative arthritis, knee problems, haemorrhoids	Red
Second (sacral)	Womb, kidneys, reproductive system, bladder, pelvic girdle, genitals. All liquids such as blood/circulatory system, lymph, gastric juices	Gonads	Impotence, frigidity, problems of uterus, bladder or kidneys, stiff lower back	Orange

Chakra	Body areas	Gland	Ailments	Colour
Third (solar plexus)	Lower back, abdomen, liver, spleen, stomach, small intestine, gall bladder, autonomic nervous system, digestive system	Pancreas	Ulcers, diabetes, hypoglycaemia, anorexia nervosa, bulimia	Yellow
Fourth (heart)	Heart, lungs, arms, hands, upper back, circulation, skin	Thymus	Asthma, high blood pressure, lung disease, heart disease	Green or pink
Fifth (throat)	Neck, shoulders, jaw, ears, bronchial tubes	Thyroid	Sore throat, stiff neck, colds, thyroid problems, hearing problems	Blue or silver
Sixth (ajna)	Eyes, two hemispheres of the brain, sinuses, face	Pituitary	Visual defects, headaches, nightmares	Indigo
Seventh (crown)	Cerebral cortex, central nervous system	Pineal	Depression, alienation, inability to learn	Pure white

will observe different shapes and rotations. If the spin is counter-clockwise it usually means that energy is being drained from that chakra instead of sending it up to the next chakra.

There are exceptions to this, however. The first is, as mentioned above, that if you are below the equator the spin is reversed. The second is that a counter-clockwise movement is commonly observed for about nine days a month in both men and women. All of us are subject to influence from celestial bodies, and the moon is a very important influence on our physical energy. Women have a 28-day menstrual cycle with some of the chakras spinning anticlockwise on about nine days of the month. Usually every other chakra will exhibit this change, and this needs to be borne in mind when working with women. It can be pinpointed by the pairs of chakras exhibiting counter-clockwise movements. This happens because the central energy meridian reverses direction during the menstrual cycle, and can be seen as the way that we eliminate incompatible energies. It is not, therefore, a sign of damage. Interestingly, men too seem to have this change every month.

The counter-clockwise spin of a chakra can also indicate damage or pathology in the organs associated with that chakra.

If the spin of the chakra is elliptical is usually means that there is something wrong energetically. It could be tiredness or it could be a malfunction of the endocrine system related to the chakra (see table on pp.102–3). Finally, it could be a problem with the lympathic system in the area of that chakra.

To become adept at viewing chakras with your guide, practise as much as possible. If someone is unwell, look at their chakras to compare them with the way they look when they are healthy.

Some channels and psychics 'see' the chakras as funnel-shaped, almost like flowers blossoming. The back of each flower is attached to a central stem (the sushumna, one of the many nadis or subtle channels in the body) which runs straight up the centre of the physical body from the first to the seventh chakra and connects them all. This is the channel up which the kundalini will rise, hence its name – channel of fire or Sarasvati.

The awakening of the kundalini occurs rarely in the West. It is the awakening of power, symbolized by a coiled snake lying in the first chakra which, when it awakens, rises to the sixth chakra. In ancient Egypt the ability to see and the awakening of psychic powers which this stimulated was sometimes depicted in a head-dress with the head of a snake – the symbol of wisdom in that culture – facing forward over the third eye or sixth chakra. As the kundalini rises up through the chakras it changes their vibration to a higher frequency, and the experience is of great bliss if the person is ready and able to surrender to it. The kundalini will not stay at the sixth and seventh chakras unless a great deal of preparation has been carried out. Sometimes it just rises through some of the chakras and falls back; it can then be very difficult to generate again for some time. Kundalini is frequently described as generating a great heat or fire in the sushumna, accompanied by trembling, uncontrollable shaking and sometimes, fear. The arousal can produce great healing if the person is open to it, but often it is traumatic and dramatic. The complete rising to the seventh chakra is said to bring enlightenment and liberation.

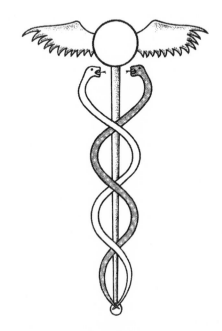

The caduceus

Around the sushumna are coiled two other nadis, the Ida and the Pingala. The Ida exits from the left of the base chakra whilst the Pingala exits from the right. They weave through the chakras forming a symmetrical pattern as seen on the caduceus, the wand of the healer, and meet at the sixth chakra, where they merge and continue upwards. If you observe a lack of symmetry in these nadis it indicates an imbalance and almost certainly a physical illness.

EXERCISE: SCANNING THE ENERGY OF THE CHAKRAS

If you can find a cooperative friend, ask them to sit in front of you for a few minutes so that you can practise scanning their energy. Begin to relax, close your eyes and bring in the energy of your guide. When you can feel the guide fully present, begin to focus on the energy of the person seated before you. Spend a few minutes pretending that you can see out of your third eye, the sixth chakra. Just focus your attention on that centre, ask your guide to open and align the centre, and then ask him to use your ability to scan to give you information about the chakras of your friend.

If you are confident in your verbal channelling begin with the first chakra and tell your friend your feelings about it, moving up from chakra to chakra until you have finished. Now ask your friend to spend a few minutes in meditation with you, focusing on the chakras and bringing them into alignment. You could use a guided meditation tape or just visualize the appropriate colour for each chakra in turn, at the same time asking the healing guides to bring the chakras into alignment and balanced function. Now scan your friend's energy again. What do you notice?

There are many variations which you can use to develop this sensing. For example, ask your friend to focus on one chakra and then deliberately bring it into balance while you scan it. Play! Practice is the way to become good at this.

You could use our tape set *Channelling for Healers* or our taped course *Working with Your Chakras* to assist with this exercise.

Auras

The spinning of the chakras creates the aura or auric field, and the amount of energy which is generated by a particular chakra or group of chakras creates the colour of the aura. The colour of the chakra itself is created by the energy which is produced by its spin – that is, its frequency. The aura is composed of layers of colour – when viewed it is like looking at a rainbow with many layers of colour, not like the aura photographs which you often find being taken at New Age fairs. However, it is important to note that this is my experience and may not be yours. Take these notes as guidance but not as direction. Each of us has our own way of perceiving subtle energies, and there is no wrong way to do it. Find your own truths and trust them.

The layers of the aura

These layers correspond to different levels of your being. The first layer, the etheric body, is close to the physical body and you can see this in what is known as Kirlian photography. This technique was developed by a Russian scientist named Semyon Kirlian. The effect created by this technique is to show a sort of energy halo which actually remains surrounding the whole leaf after a piece of leaf has been torn off. Kirlian believed that this effect was the aura of the leaf. Kirlian photographs of a hand also show the luminescence of the aura.

The etheric body directly reflects what is happening in the physical body; it feeds on the energies transmuted by the chakras and can be affected by meditation, breathing and visualizations. Because this first layer is associated with the first chakra it plays an important part in the amount of energy that is accessible to the individual – it is often said that this layer is the 'blueprint' for the physical form. It usually extends only a couple of inches from the body, is frequently perceived as being a bluey grey colour, and pulses.

The second layer or the emotional body will give you a lot of information about the person's current emotional state. It is about three inches out from the physical body and is moving all the time. This is like aura photographs with clouds of colour. It contains all colours, and the chakras look like their typical colours within it.

The third layer, the mental body, is usually yellow which is the colour of thinking. Sometimes other colours come in, but they are usually the emotions associated with the thoughts going on at the time, so that you are observing an entanglement of emotional and mental body issues.

OBSERVATIONS

When I tune in with Ortan I can always tell whether someone has been doing work on themselves. When I channel I always scan energy first: those who have been meditating and working on connecting with the higher aspects of themselves frequently have a lot of white and gold light in the upper areas of their aura. Sometimes you can see the flow of energy up through the crown chakra like a fountain of light, especially in those with awakened Light Bodies – people who are fully awakened at a spiritual level.

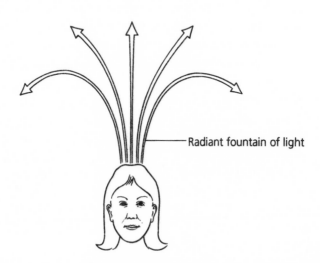

Radiant fountain of light

Those who are manifesting a strong connection with the soul or the higher self will often have from the top of the head a highly visible antakarana – a channel that connects the lower self to the soul, to the monad and higher. I often 'see' this as gold or whitish-gold, with soft, pulsating light moving down it and into the crown chakra.

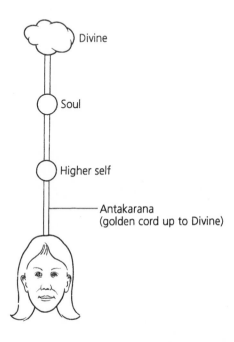

Physical illnesses are usually visible within the body – so, for example, if someone comes with a back problem I might see the problem but usually also feel it in my own body. I don't feel the actual symptoms but I get a strong feeling that these areas are not flowing. It might feel like an ache or a coldness in my own body as I channel. When you then 'look' at the person's energy there is a darkness and a greyness in these areas of the aura or the body, often both. Cancers look very dark, almost like holes in the energy, and the solar plexus chakra is almost always very weak, as is the base chakra.

When one lady came for a reading with us I could clearly see a dark area around her right breast and shoulder/arm joint areas. Ortan asked if she had any problems in this area and she said she didn't. I surmised that perhaps this was something that had not yet manifested in the physical body, so I gently questioned her after the reading. She suddenly smiled and said, 'Oh, of course I did have breast cancer a few years ago which resulted in a mastectomy and the removal of the lymph nodes under the arm.'

Sometimes the questions people ask don't necessarily appear to be about health or chakras at all, but when you tune in with your guide it is very clear where the problems lie. In one reading the lady asked about why she was so easily put down by other people, and how she could get over this problem. First of all Ortan pointed out that she needed to learn to trust herself, emphasizing that trust was an important thing for her to experience at this point of her journey through life. He went on to talk about her second and third chakras, saying that they were out of balance and alignment. He gave her practical things that she could do to correct the problem, such as using Reiki (a form of healing where the practitioner channels the Reiki energy through the hands to assist the client's healing process) into the chakras and also working with crystals. Finally he told her that meditation with the chakras would be very useful for building her confidence.

9

COMMON QUESTIONS ABOUT CHANNELLING

We guides have an independent existence. It is our joy to serve you, to play with you and to work with you when you are ready to do so.

ORTAN

Over the years that I have been teaching channelling certain types of question are asked very often, and in order to assist you a number of these are answered below. Remember that you can also ask your guide's advice if you have questions.

PHYSICAL SYMPTOMS FROM CHANNELLING

QUESTIONER: After we contacted our guides I found that as I came back from the meditation I was really hot. Is this normal?
LITA: Very! I still get very hot when I am channelling, and so do many channels I know. What happens when you channel is that you change your rate of vibration to match that of your guide. Imagine that we are all vibrating at a certain rate, that all our atoms are vibrating at that frequency. As you increase the frequency it is as if things are speeding up as you hold more and more energy. This combination of increasing your vibration and holding more energy is felt at the physical level as heat. You may find, as you work with your guide, that you get more accustomed to his or her vibratory rate and don't experience so much heat.

When I am giving readings for people I still always experience some heat, and it is extremely strong when my guide channels healing energy for them. Ortan often beams energy to our clients, and this is very hot work! The client, however, often experiences this not as heat but as light.

QUESTIONER: My neck really aches after channelling my guide. What can I do?
LITA: First check that you don't need any treatment such as osteopathy. If your spinal alignment is all right, there are two main things to think about.

The first is your posture. It is important to be very upright when you channel, with your back straight and your head placed as if a line could be drawn down from the top of your head down through the spine. Tuck your chin in slightly as if to accentuate a double chin.

The second important area is the centre at the back of your head and neck, where you may need more flow. Spend a few moments gently nodding your head to find the position where the back of your neck feels easy and relaxed and no strain is placed on it.

If you still experience discomfort of any type ask your guide about the problem. Perhaps you need to surrender at a physical level even more, or to pay attention to your physical body in some way – you may need to take more or less exercise, or perhaps change your diet.

QUESTIONER: My health isn't good. Does that exclude me from being able to channel a guide?
ORTAN: *No. Indeed your health would improve if you channelled a guide, for the guide energy running through the body will improve the frequency. There are problems with your chest, are there not?*
QUESTIONER: Yes, I'm told that I'm hyperventilating. One of the latest problems is anxiety states.
ORTAN: *Yes, you have tightness in the chest and difficulty with the breath, and this is very clear in your energy. There are many ways that you could shift this problem, dear one. Do you go to a healer? [Ortan went on to give suggestions for improving the questioner's physical condition.]*

BLOCKING THE INFORMATION

QUESTIONER: I often wonder if I'm interfering with my guide in the sense that when I make the contact I feel he wants to speak, but he never starts to talk unless somebody asks a question, whether it be myself mentally or somebody else. I wondered why this was.

ORTAN: *It is a basic law of the universe that you must ask. Guides will never thrust any information or knowledge upon you, however high it may be. So your guide, eager though he may be to assist you, will not do so unless you ask.*

QUESTIONER: I got the book a long time ago and tried some of the work at home. It shows me something that I should be doing, but there's something blocking me from doing it. Yet it seems it's a natural thing for me to be able to do.

ORTAN: *Yes, so it is.*

QUESTIONER: Well, I want to know what to do about that.

ORTAN: *All that will be blocking you is your personality. All the other levels of your being will be keen to channel. Channelling is normal – a natural thing for humans to do, is it not? But you have been given many warnings and worries about why you cannot channel, and who can and who can't – all of these funny stories that are spread on your earth plane about channelling.*

Of course, some people make better verbal channels than others. Some people are channels for guides who work with art, with music, with all sorts of others areas, and your guides will be aligned with your life's purpose. So my suggestion to you would be to really work at finding your life's purpose, your path of joy and love and growth. As you move on to that, the channelling will become easy because then the guides will be able to come through strongly.

Also important is to spend at least twenty to thirty minutes a day in meditation, keeping the mind completely clear, keeping the body in discipline, calm, relaxed, mind focused and alert, clear like a mountain stream, like a lake, so that the impressions of your higher self, your guide and your teachers on the inner planes can come through to

you without struggle, rather than having to beat their way through in
the night in your dreams. This will really improve your ability to
connect in with the higher realms.

LITA: We find that many people ask about being blocked in
different ways. The easiest thing is just to work on feeling the
connection first and not worrying too much about actual verbal
channelling. Our processes on the *Channelling for Healers* tape
course will help with this – the focus is on connecting with a
guide who is aligned with your higher purpose. All the processes
are based on meditation techniques and so you can accomplish
two things at once – developing the connection with your guide
and practising meditation. Remember, too, that your natural
anxiety may be blocking you. Relaxing the body, as well as the
meditation practice suggested above by Ortan, is very helpful in
allowing you to work with this anxiety.

QUESTIONER: In a reading I was given the name of a guide. I
call on all sorts of guides anyway but I don't really seem to be
getting the feedback. It always seems as though I have got to keep
making up my own mind – it's always down to me. I don't get
anything coming through so that I can say, 'I will do that.'
ORTAN: *It is a question of free will, is it not? Do you wish to live*
your life by your choice or by the choice of another entity? And of
course you need to live your life by your own choices and you don't
channel a guide until you have the strength to understand that which
you most certainly have now, do you not?

So part of the difficulty with this experience of guide advice or
information has been to do with your learning to trust yourself and
your own perceptions, to trust your own ability, to guide your own life
in the correct way, because you have had times when you have leaned
on others and it was not appropriate. And so the support is not given,
if you like, so that you will be able to integrate this lesson. But there is
certainly a guide present in your aura at this time that we are aware
of. And now what you need to do is to learn to still the mind even
more, to let the mind be even clearer.

But part of the problem for you is that your ability is not going to be as a verbal channel. Your ability will be to channel different types of material, and for this reason you do not get clear words in your mind always. You will get impressions and feelings, you will have felt a sense of the correct path or the correct choice to make, and there may be other ways that you can bring guidance through that are very accurate, dear one, and are simply an easier route for your particular energy to bring. You have a very strong energy, do you not, a very vigorous energy, and this enables you to contact beings of a very particular nature. But they are not very verbal.

NOT HEARING VOICES

QUESTIONER: I don't hear things, I just. . . .

ORTAN: *No. You just know.*

QUESTIONER: Yes.

ORTAN: *It is a knowingness. Very few humans hear things. If you think about the people on your earth plane who hear things, they are the mad people, they are the schizophrenic people who are hearing voices. They are not true voices, they are simply a stimulation of a part of their brain – it sounds like a voice to them.*

Channelling is not like that. It is subtle. You will notice that Orin and DaBen's [other guides] teachings on how to channel are very subtle. It is finding the difference between one thing and another – some very similar thing to another. The subtlety of channelling and perhaps the challenge of it is that initially the shift when you bring in the guide is so familiar that you think it is not true.

WHAT SHOULD WE CHANNEL?

QUESTIONER: Is it important to know who you're talking to, as it were?

ORTAN: *Yes. There is importance in the sense that we recommend that you work to connect with high-level beings. There are beings on your astral plane, which is the next level of reality to your earth reality, very close to earth, and a repository for many dead souls as they travel through the higher dimensions. The astral plane has many difficult energies, playful and mischievous – not dangerous, but they could be very uncomfortable to work with. They are very misleading and manifest where people are unguarded – where people are not always attuned to the highest, shall we say. Now astral entities gain power from your energy, so once you connect in with them they can drain you very much; they can really take a lot of your energy if you give it. So the important thing is not to dabble or play with lower frequencies of the astral plane.*

Now the easiest way to make a connection with that plane, of course, is through the games on your earth plane like the ouija boards. We do not recommend this form of activity, because it is such an open channel for astral mischief. And so it is important to know the level of the being with whom you work. The identity can be more tricky, but it is the level, that is what I would strongly recommend you to look at.

QUESTIONER: There are many people at the moment who are channelling beings that call themselves the 'ascended masters', and I wonder if you could explain who these masters are and their purposes.

ORTAN: *Indeed. We have come to a time upon the earth plane where your planet has become of great interest. The changes that are occurring for your planet, the ascension of your planet, the evolution of your planet and all those who ride upon it, is an important move, if you like, within the divine plan, if you wish to call it that. Ascended masters are a particular type of energy, a very high energy. Those who are channelling these masters in many cases are making a genuine connection to masters of light. 'Ascended masters' is simply a term in the sense that they are ascended into another dimension, not the third in which you reside.*

These ascended masters are given various guises and they are seen in different ways according to the beliefs of the channel, according to their upbringing and their ability to encompass the energy of the master. For each channel can encompass a certain amount of energy, a certain range of frequencies, and so some people find that they are very aligned to this particular set of frequencies.

I'M MAKING IT ALL UP

QUESTIONER: I think that the problem with me is that I find it difficult to believe what I see or what I hear. Am I making it up? Is it all in my mind. Is it true?

ORTAN: *It is all in your mind – where else can it be? Because this is the only sensing mechanism that you have, and because it is in your mind, it seems like it is your thoughts, does it not? And it is difficult to distinguish between your fantasies and something that is coming in from the outside. That is why discernment is an important frequency.*

QUESTIONER: Can you tell me what guides I'm working with at the moment? I feel my work is with Sananda. I choose to call him Sananda because it takes it away from Jesus and the Orthodox Church which I've rather drifted away from, and his essence is very precious to me. And so sometimes I wonder if I think I'm making the connection – whether in fact I am or whether it's just wishful thinking.

ORTAN: *The energy of the great teachers is always present on the inner planes, and these great teachers have numbered quite a few over the thousands of years that they have been choosing to manifest on the earth plane. Take Sananda and Buddha, for example: the essence energy of these kinds of teachers is always present because they have chosen to stay in service for humanity – they have chosen to be accessible and close. They have chosen this work – it is part of their mission, their higher purpose if you like, to do this. It is therefore not difficult to connect in with their energy, and the ease with which you can do this can be concerning. (Am I making it up? How could it be so easy?)*

But you are right; you are making a connection with this energy. This is the nature of the great teachers of the earth plane – to be access-ible, not to be remote. What help could they be then if you could not contact their energy? So they must be close. They are like us, always present because where we live, where we exist, we are beyond time. We do not mind being called at two in the morning; we are not asleep. This consciousness of Sananda is ongoing and omnipresent. It is an energy into which you can tap and draw energy from if you wish to, and you know that. You have felt that, and this is real perception.

QUESTIONER: Good. I hoped it wasn't a delusion.

ORTAN: *No because delusion is a problem for those on the earth plane. There are many traps on the path that you can fall into, and you are right to be careful. It is important to be discerning, to be careful what you are doing, and not to fall prey to ego.*

QUESTIONER: Is it possible for you to tell me which guides I am working with or who are working with me at present? Can you identify them to some extent for me?

ORTAN: *At this moment there are three guides working closely into your energy. The first we will call female – she's not female, but if you were to perceive her you would call her that. We will always make this polarity, because you are in a world of polarity. This guide is a guide of joy, laughter and fun. She wishes you to be light, to embrace a life of happiness. She is a guide who has been called in specifically by you in some of the work you have done. You have particularly, if you like, invoked her energy. Of the other two guides one is quite a powerful healing guide, and the other one has the energy of a communicator, of one who heals through communication, who is discursive. If you choose to channel verbally, this is the guide you would channel.*

QUESTIONER: I'd love to do some channelling.

ORTAN: *You wouldn't have a problem channelling that guide – he will speak a great deal. I won't give you names, because the names of guides are merely frequencies – call signs, if you like – and the way that you perceive the frequency of the names of your guides may be different, according to how they wish you to call them. And we don't like to take the joy of that connection away from you.*

QUESTIONER: I have been told not to channel on my own because it's not safe.

ORTAN: *But you are never alone when you channel, dear one, you cannot channel without your guide. It is always safe to channel with your guide. Your guide is here to love and protect you. You have made a connection with a high-level guide. You are not alone when you are channelling, dear one. How could that be?*

QUESTIONER: I think I meant in the human form.

ORTAN: *Well, channel with your dog, with your cat, with your goldfish – this would be fun, would it not? (We are teasing with you, dear one! You must forgive us.) But it is difficult to conceive of channelling alone. Whenever you open to channel, your guide is protecting you. Often there will be many angels about you, other beings. It is difficult to be alone in this universe.*

Do you find yourself – I will be serious – do you find yourself becoming fearful when you are alone and channelling?

QUESTIONER: Never.

ORTAN: *Then there is not a problem. Does that answer the question, though, dear one?*

QUESTIONER: Yes, because I want to get on with the channelling. I feel that I get really good results, and I must admit it's more fun when it's just the two of us.

ORTAN: *It is important when you're channelling, dear one, to spend a moment to dedicate it to the highest good of your soul before you begin, to connect with God, with the angels, and to call your guide, so that you are working at the highest possible vibration.*

QUESTIONER: I have recently been asked why I want to channel, and it was suggested that it's perhaps an ego trip. The problem is I don't really know how to answer these people because I don't know why I want to channel – it's just something instinctive.

ORTAN: *Indeed. And we could say that the reason you are not able to access your wishes in a coherent way so that you can defend yourself is because it is your higher self, dear one, that calls you to channel. It is not your lower self, as we call it, your personality self. It is the higher aspect of yourself that wishes you to channel. Very often those who come to us who wish to learn to channel, will say, 'We do not know why we are here. We do not know why we wish to do this.' And, dear one, this is because you are making a direct connection with the higher aspects of your being.*

The reasoning, the thinking patterns of these higher aspects of yourself, are not necessarily accessible, but they will be following the mission, the dictate, if you like, of your soul, and this is why you are drawn to channel.

Many people upon the earth plane are learning to channel at this time because of the changes that have been occurring for humanity in the past few years, the changes that are known as the 'dawning of the new age'. With the dawning of this age, the frequencies that are bombarding your planet are shifting and changing. This shift is leading to more awareness of the spiritual dimension of life, and those of you who are more to the forefront of this movement, those who are destined in the long term to be the leaders of this movement, and those who assist others in their growth, must learn to channel, for by channelling you are drawing directly on the wisdom of the higher realms, not on the opinions and thoughts of the lower realms. This is an important shift in humanity's ability to bring through higher knowledge and higher wisdom, is it not.

CHANNELLING VISUALLY

QUESTIONER: When I was asked, as my guide, if there were any areas on the physical body that had any blockages, at that point I actually saw what I call a clairvoyant picture, which is often what I receive during healing. My guide then interpreted that picture. Is that just a normal part of channelling? What do you see when you are channelling?

LITA: Yes – that's what I see as well. If somebody asks about the physical body, my vision shifts immediately and it becomes very visual. I see their energy system and their aura, I see areas where there are blockages and others where there aren't. I see areas where there are imbalances, where there's disease.

If someone, for example, comes with a particular disease I can usually tune right into where it is. But I'm not a doctor, so I'm very careful with my guide about how we work on that. I've learnt now over the years to trust the way that Ortan will discuss that kind of thing. And very often people already know what's the matter with them, and as soon as you say something they say, 'Oh yes, I have had this problem,' and then it goes from there.

GUIDES, HIGHER SELF AND SOUL

QUESTIONER: I wondered whether you could clarify the difference between the guides, the higher self and the soul.

ORTAN: *It is a problem on the earth plane, is it not? Let's start with guides. We are not part of you in the way that the higher self and the soul are. We guides have an independent existence. It is our joy to serve you, to play with you and to work with you when you are ready to do so.*

There are many definitions of all of the different aspects of yourself. Let's begin at the beginning. You have a physical vehicle that you have chosen for this lifetime but the presence within the physical vehicle – your personality and the things that operate the physical vehicle, if you like – are just the tip of the iceberg. Your entirety, your entire self as an energy being, is a great deal more complex – you could say larger – than that which is manifested through the physical vehicle. The physical vehicle is an extension of your consciousness. It is where your consciousness has focused for this short time to learn lessons, to have experiences, to do other things that are part of the higher purpose, in other words part of the agenda of the larger being. This larger being exists through the dimensions and into the higher dimensions, and these are the aspects which we are discussing when we are talking of higher self – we are talking of soul, of monad.

The level of higher self is often confused on the earth plane with the term 'soul'. We would draw a distinction between these two aspects of your energy. We are talking about existence at different vibrational frequencies – or different dimensional levels. The higher self is very close to the physical self, being an aspect of your energy that is very close to physical reality, and the higher self can therefore mediate between the physical vehicle, the personality, and the lower self and the higher aspects of the soul. So it is not a problem to use the terms 'higher self' and 'soul' interchangeably. But the reality is that the soul is at a higher, pure frequency and is aligned directly with the emanations of Source, of Divine Creator, via the monad, of the All That Is the centre of what is emanating manifested beings, which is emanating souls, which is emanating the universe or possibilities in other words of existence.

10

FOCUSED EXTRACTS FROM GUIDES

We can teach you of many topics if you wish to learn of them.

ORTAN

This chapter consists mostly of channellings by Lita with her guides Ortan and Shalaya on a variety of topics.

ON CHANNELLING

ORTAN: *For this process of change or fluctuation in life as you make the connection to the higher realms can be very dangerous. It threatens the personality. It threatens the ego. It threatens all of the things that humans try so desperately to maintain. For by being born in a physical body they then start to become embedded in that physical reality, and have forgotten by the time they are adults who and what they truly are. And when they are children any remembrances are often ridiculed or misunderstood, for children are not good at communicating. And it is difficult for them to put over complicated ideas, for they only see parts of the idea and when it is presented in this way it appears illogical.*

And so, as adults, channelling is that route back to finding out who and what you really are, to discovering more about your higher purpose, about your soul and your path of growth. For the guide is attuned to all of these things and can give you information about them if you wish it. But most of all this connection moves light, and light in its natural form will always flow. And when it is unable to flow it will create build-up, and these build-ups will always have to keep moving until they find another way to flow, for light and love have to flow. Flow and fluidity are one of the natural states of all things in the universe.

QUESTIONER: I wanted to ask about how we, as new channels, can be aware of our personal stuff affecting the information.

ORTAN: *That is a good question, dear one. One of the greatest challenges of being a channel in a physical body is the challenge of the involvement of the ego and the personality. In order to detect whether ego is getting in the way is very difficult for you, especially when you are beginning to channel, because you are going through 'Is it me? Is it a guide? What is going on here?'*

And for this reason it is most important in the development of your work as a channel that you take care to spend a lot of time working through the most basic levels of your beingness. And when I talk of these levels I am talking of physical level, of emotional level, of psychological level, spiritual level too. But each level requires your attention and your rigorous mindfulness in some of the disciplines on the earth plane. In Buddhism there is a construct of mindfulness, of being present in the moment and observing oneself at all times.

This practice of centring into mindfulness is the most important and useful practice that you as a channel can develop. Mindfulness extends from the physical body, because if the physical body is not clear, then you will not be a good channel. It extends through the emotional body, and this is carried out through therapy, through psychotherapy, through NLP techniques, whichever technique draws you. It is important that you dissolve and release those clusters of beliefs, of emotions and of things that will trigger your material, that will trigger your emotional reactions. And when you're channelling you will feel some of those reactions, will you not? You will feel fear or surprise or disgust – this is when you must be careful and get out of the way.

So clearing yourself is the easiest way for this not to occur, and this clearing is part of the path of spiritual growth. And so channelling takes you on the path of spiritual growth at all levels. But it has to come to the physical. You are a physical being. It must come to the emotional, for the nature of physical being is emotion.

ON THE EFFECTS OF CHANNELLING AT THIS TIME

This channelling came through as we were setting the energies for an Opening to Channel class on 11 May 1996.

ORTAN: *Notice that some of the members of this group's guides are those who are here to hold the frequencies of the new changes. Notice the difference in the frequencies of the guides that you are meeting – some of these guides have been incarnated upon the earth plane, and risen through the realms to become great masters of light. Notice that the guides are as assorted as the human people are, but all have one thing in common, that they resonate to the frequency of this time, that they resonate to the frequencies of love and compassion, that they will raise the vibration of the channels they have chosen, they will shift their lives in ways they cannot begin to guess. They will open their hearts to these frequencies, to their higher path and higher purpose on the earth plane. And they will bring much comfort as well, for some of these human people are very lonely and in need, great need of comfort, of support in their lives, for the changes are not easy to integrate.*

ON THE PURPOSE OF CHANNELLING

ORTAN: *Why channel? What is in channelling for humans and for guides? For guides it is a way for them to bring information to the earth plane. And this benefit is also a benefit for those who are the channels. Channels reaching to these realms are opening doorways all over the planet. And as that focus of openness between the realms is increasingly held by more and more channels you can see that the difference between the realms becomes less in a sense. For there are more passageways both ways from our realms to yours and from your realms to ours. And by opening the doorways, in time all the doorways will stay open, and then very much more information will be taken by channels, even those who are not so practised. And so for channels it is a chance to be in service simply to make the connection. . . .*

    Throughout the history of humanity individuals have channelled. Channelling is normal. Guidance from the higher realms is useful and needed. But the most important use of channelling is to empower individuals to trust in the beauty and reality of the light. To know that there is a God that they are part of and who is part of them. For them to realize that they are souls upon the earth plane and to know that their earth plane reality is simply another phase in their existence.

On the Nature of Channels

ORTAN: *We are often asked whether everybody can channel, whether there is a guide for every human being, and the answer is yes. All human beings have the ability to channel, because all human beings are souls upon the earth plane. But if they have not chosen before this lifetime to work with these frequencies, if they are on a different path of growth, then they will not channel. It is not because they cannot, but because it is not their chosen path in this lifetime.*

On Guides and Where They are

ORTAN: *I am dwelling in a form which to you would appear perhaps as simply a shimmer, as a movement within the air. You are unable to see me with your eyes or to hear me with your ears. And as we are in our dimension and in this place of light, there is little that I can tell you about this dimension that would have any meaning for you.*

I can tell you that we are here in service to the divine. I can tell you that we have a community, and that we communicate and work together, and that many of us have evolved from beings that have been incarnated both on the earth plane and in other places. Some of us have pledged to work with humanity to assist mankind with awakening to the light and the love that is the true reality of God or the divine or the source – whatever you wish to call that energy. We serve that energy in joy, for it is our place to do the bidding of the divine.

So where we are, dear one, is what you might term another dimension. A dimension of light, a dimension in which there is no physical reality, for we are in a dimension that is full of light, of frequencies of love, of service. We are in a place where everything is manifest immediately, and thus if we think of something it is reality. And this is a very joyous place for us to be, and we are all connected together energetically as if we are one, as indeed all beings are connected.

There is no difference between any being and any other being in some senses, and yet each is a star or a spark of the divine energy and has a unique role to play in the evolution of the universe. But it is well to remember that all came from the divine, and in time all will return to this source of light and of love. Love and light are the basic frequencies of God or the divine, and it is our joy to serve these frequencies. Our realms are reached through many layers; if you like, you might see them as planes or as layers or as dimensions – these are all terms to try to describe the energetic differences between these places. And indeed all the souls that pass over in death move first to one plane, and we have called it the astral plane. But it is of no matter what you call it, and from this plane they rise as they are ready through other planes. There are many on our side to assist in this process. You are not alone; you are always supported and cared for.

QUESTIONER: What manner of being are you?

SHALAYA: *Well, I am a being – just as you are in essence. I am a focus of vibration, a place of location, of vibration. I am simply one who chooses to step forward and be able to bring information to you. I have no physical existence. I am difficult for your kind to under-stand because I am a being of light and vibration and I have no form. I do not especially have an interest in manipulation of matter because . . . we can see that difficulties are caused by this matter, physicality, manifestation, existence, and we have been fortunate in our evolution that we have not had to descend to the third dimension. We are not bounded by space or time or matter or any of these aspects of your existence.*

So I am a being, into communication with you when it is required, and you could say that I have no independent existence. I do have an independent existence, but not in the way that you understand it.

For our race has very little need of physical movement, since we are able now to project our consciousness out over time and space and therefore we are not anchored to a physical existence. You could say we have in some senses transcended some of the cycles that you are still wound within, cycles of death and rebirth. For when a race becomes evolved beyond a certain point then there is choice for each member in these matters. But your race has not come to this point, and your race will not come to this point yet. It is not relevant in some ways to be concerned about these matters.

And we come simply to bring in these other frequencies, anchoring them through the dimensions and the spans, for we have become expert in this matter. And you ask what I am called, and my name is Shalaya. And this is just the resonance of my frequency, but it is of no importance either to me or to you. I do not have a polarity for we do not reproduce, we have no need to do this, for all our souls have already been brought into being. So the way that we would choose to be conscious has already been done.

ON PERSONAL GUIDES

ORTAN: There are personal guides who help people through their lives. It is to be understood that all guides work together and these guides work at a more individual level. Whilst my work with Lita has been fairly individual you will have noticed that right from the beginning I have been teaching others and making connections to others, calling them in for you [Lita] to work with. Other types of guides do not do this. They assist the individual in their personal development. They are not there to work with others. And so many people that you would have taught opening to channel to will have personal guides for themselves only. There is nothing wrong with this and these guides are very interesting.

ON TRANSCENSION GUIDES

These words came from Ortan channelling for this book on 10 and 21 August 1995.

ORTAN: There are guides who are specifically here to serve humanity's transcension, which you call ascension, and others that are not. I, for example, am a guide serving humanity's transcension. But some guides are connecting into the higher purpose of the person, and *these guides are often in fact the person's higher self and not a guide in the true form. So it is first of all important to make the distinction, for the person channelling will not always be aware of the difference. For they too are guides. You are all guides in potential, although you are not presently guides, if you see what I mean. And so in ascending on the soul planes you will eventually reach the plane of guides and masters, teachers and so on. Some guides such as myself who are transcension guides also work on a plane with the masters, and we are considered masters by some. For we are here to teach and bring information. We store ancient wisdoms. . . .*

And it also occurs to me to say that when I have talked to you about types of guides you must not consider that guides have only one function and that transcension guides are only transcension guides. This would be their main purpose, but they may have other things that they do. So do not find this too rigid. . . .

ORTAN: *Transcension guides are those who are going to assist humanity in transcending and ascending. We call it transcension as a shorthand. Transcension is about ascending and transcending these limitations of the present reality and transforming and transmuting it into another reality. Which will still be to do with the earth plane, but it will be at a different frequency or resonance if you like because the shifts that will occur will change the energy of those who are to stay and transcend. So the transcension guides are those who are here for that process, to teach and guide those who come through this process as one group.*

ON HEALING

Ortan had this to say in response to a question about whether it was acceptable to be a channel for healing energy when that energy was not the questioner's own.

ORTAN: *Of course, dear one. It is a beautiful path, is it not, and we need many, many healers at this time, and many are awakening to their healing abilities. Your ability to heal is a gift that you have been given in this lifetime. Use it, dear one, use it generously and with love, and it will bring much growth for you. And you are quite right to say that it is not your energy, for how could you as a human heal anything? It is God who moves through you, is it not? And it is a gift and it is a joy to do this, for all humans have the ability to channel this healing energy. But it is their choice whether or not they will serve God in this way.*

ON THE WORK OF ANGELS

This is a transcript of a conversation with an angel called Samuel, channelled by a friend of Lita's named Jennie, who chose to assist with the writing of this book.

LITA: Samuel, are you from the light?
JENNIE/SAMUEL: *Indeed I am from the light. This is the first time I have spoken through a channel. I am an angel. I do not have a physical shape.*

LITA: Can you tell us where the angels live? Where are you now?
JENNIE/SAMUEL: *A very high mountain of light.*

LITA: Are there many of you there?
JENNIE/SAMUEL: *Collectively there are many of us.*

LITA: Hundreds or thousands or millions?
JENNIE/SAMUEL: *Tens of millions.*

LITA: What sort of work are these angels doing? Are they all doing the same work, or different work?
JENNIE/SAMUEL: *Some are doing different work, but I am bringing the healing rays into your world.*

LITA: Have you been doing this for some time?
JENNIE/SAMUEL: *While there has been light.*

LITA: Samuel, are there many of you bringing the healing rays to the earth?

JENNIE/SAMUEL: *There are several of us. We are angels of light. We are all from the light. I am not an archangel.*

LITA: What do archangels do?
JENNIE/SAMUEL: *Archangels serve the divine master. They are directly connected to the source. I am a bringer of the healing rays. I am on a path of progression also.*

LITA: What happens as you move along this path?
JENNIE/SAMUEL: *The light gets brighter still.*

LITA: You say that you are a bringer of the healing rays. Can you tell us how you do this?
JENNIE/SAMUEL: *It is simply through love.*

ON CARING FOR OUR PHYSICAL BODIES

ORTAN: *Nothing is too trivial or too small to be discussed. The physical side is just as important as the personality side in the beginning. Encourage them [those for whom you channel] to discuss what it is that they do to support the physical body. And support them in making changes to this so that the body will work fluidly and well for many years, that they may support their spiritual development. Do not allow them to consider these things unimportant and do not allow yourself to consider them trivial. For if one comes forward who is unwell or who is overweight, or who is not exercising or eating well, then support them to make this first change.*

For those who abuse the body are those who are not in self-love, for you would not abuse your body. If you loved it you could not do this. Learn to tune into the body and listen to its requirements. . . .

So we return to the topic of love and self-love. In order to recognize the type of being that you truly are, it is important to know exactly what it is that you are. That you understand the physical side and you love it. For your bodies are the way that spirit is manifested on the earth plane and they must be nurtured and cared for very tenderly so that they do not distract spirit from this work. Hence it is of no importance for you to spend time concerning yourselves about the looks of these bodies but very much more about the workings of these bodies. And it is for this reason that we counsel exercise and dietary changes. Not because we wish to assist you in the ego practice of vanity but because we wish to assist you in growth. So do not concern yourself if the body is growing a little heavier than it has been in the past, for there is no danger to your health – and it is the health side that we consider to be so important. . . .

So loving the body will bring health to the body and by following the practice of smiling that you have been shown by the very enlightened Thich Nat Hanh you can enhance your health even more. Use this practice, smiling to every organ of the body, to every part of the body, as a regular meditation.

ON CONNECTING WITH THE HIGHEST POSSIBLE GUIDE

ORTAN: *And so we do consider it important that the channel makes a choice consciously to ask for the highest-level guide that it is possible for them to work with. Because by doing this, both the guides and the channels will be assured of the most productive relationship. Because a channel channelling a guide who is not of the highest level of energy they can hold will not be challenged, will not be stretched. Their energy will not expand, working with a lower-level guide. The higher-level guide, on the other hand, will be able to bring the channel through to new experience, to new insight and new knowledge, to different perspectives, higher perspectives.*

ON THE UNTAPPED RESOURCES OF THE HUMAN BRAIN

ORTAN: *And it has often been remarked upon by those on the earth plane that there is a great deal of the human brain that is unused, and of course there is. For there are many abilities that human beings have that are as yet untapped, and all these parts of the brain await activation. And one of the things that this part of the brain is used for is channelling, for it gives a broader base, if you like, for the reception of intuition. And another reason that this part of brain is not used is that you have all not awakened your healing abilities. And yet just as every human can channel, so can every human heal.*

ON WAYS IN WHICH GUIDES COMMUNICATE KNOWLEDGE

ORTAN: *And it is important that you continue to read and be open to all that is occurring around you, sifting in this information to the human brain. To allow us access to even more information upon the earth plane that we may spread more clear information to those who wish to hear this.*

We can teach you of many topics if you wish to learn of them. We do not always do this directly. It is sometimes by giving you information on the earth plane, allowing your energies to find the correct information easily. So sometimes we will tell you things and other times we will ensure the books, the people and so on are delivered to you. And it is better you do not have too much expectation of how this may occur, for guides work according to the easiness of the energy.

And we also do not consider it to be useful to channel persons who have died, unless they have evolved to a point where they are starting to make conscious decisions, because they can become confused about whether they are dead or alive. And as you know, the ego is something that can continue beyond death in the sense that the being is not yet evolved enough to realize that it is interconnected, that it is a part of the divine, that it is of no importance. Some material can be channelled that may not be so helpful for those upon the earth plane, although the reasons for this are not perhaps what you may think. But there is a tendency by those beings on the earth plane to hold channelled information in reverence, to consider that every word that is spoken is correct, and you know that this is not true. And I know that it is difficult to send the information to you in a way that is beyond ambiguity.

On the Perceptions Developed through Channelling

ORTAN: *You are able to see a certain spectrum of frequency, to hear a certain vibratory frequency, to feel the nature of these frequencies through the skin and the touch. And also you have other sense perceptions which are developing, which rely on understanding the inner nature of some of these vibratory subtleties. For they move into another dimension which you are starting to perceive.*

On Calling Other Guides

ORTAN: *A human can always say no to a guide, and so this channel could refuse to channel my energies, and that would be all right. The human may then call a different guide to them. And it is not to say that this guide would be lower. It may be of the same level, but a different type of information [would be] brought by that guide. For example, if the channel wished suddenly to become an expert upon a certain subject then it would be appropriate for the channel to call a guide who knows about this subject to assist. And I would be happy to assist in making that connection. We are not jealous of our channels.*

On Connections between Channels and Guides

ORTAN: *We notice you are also confused about this question of many people channelling one guide, and you know that it is true that I work with many, many individuals. But I do not allow myself to be verbally channelled by any other individuals, and if they try they find that they are unable to do it. They will attribute different reasons to this, and these are not important – these are simply the rationalizations of their mind. But the reason we have chosen this particular way to do this is that the channel who is present upon the earth plane and I have had connections before. And for this reason it is easier for us to work together. These previous connections mean that we have much that we have already sorted out energetically between us, and so this makes it all much simpler.*

ORTAN: *Is there anything you wish to ask about Marco at this time?*
MARCO: I think most people will be extremely interested to know if you and the channel have worked together before this lifetime. Can you enlarge a little bit about that? Do guides and humans work together through incarnations?
ORTAN: *Oh, indeed. The guide and the human may work together for many lifetimes if their energy is compatible and there is more they can achieve together. And we often teach another soul for many years, for the teacher–student relationship is not a short-term one. And my work with the channel and many of my students is not a short-term project, so to speak. But this particular channel and I have [had] energy consonance before. She has lived a meditative life as a male upon the earth plane before. And in this life, this meditative life, the guides were all about all of those who lived at that time. And it was quite normal and she then channelled me. Although she was considered to be a teacher herself, even though she was a male to confuse you, but she channelled me and we taught together. And in those times channelling was something that was not discussed, it was normal. All teachers channelled guides to assist them, and in many traditions this is quite normal – not just upon the earth plane. This link between the realms is an essential qualification for teachers. For if they have not access to higher energy and higher wisdom, then how can they teach?*

ON THE EGO

ORTAN: *And this question of ego is an important issue, an issue of great relevance for channels. For it is easy to believe that because one is a channel then one is a great being. But what is important to recall is that the channel is one whose path is to do this. And you may like to consider that you could judge channels by the nature of the beings that they choose to channel. You could consider that this might be an indicator of the energy of the channel and this connection between guide and channel is an energetic connection, one where the energies are consonant.*

ON DYING AND REINCARNATION

ORTAN: *When you die you don't just disappear into nothingness. This does not occur, unless you have a very strong belief that that is what does occur, in which case you could spin for a bit before you are picked up. When you die there is assistance in the transition. Your guide, of course, you've already connected in with. There are angels, there are souls who make a point of being there when people die, so that when the transition occurs they can gently let an orientation occur. Just as when you go into meditation and you orientate your inner vision, when you die it is a similar kind of thing. You orientate to your death experience and you orientate to your beingness without a physical body. You've been in a physical body for a bit, you'll soon be relieved to be out of it. When you die you start to feel some joy, real joy. But there will be a time of integration, of resting, quite often for a soul, of lessons to be integrated, of time spent in learning and developing and growing. Not all our growth is done from the earth plane; it can be done without a physical body a lot more easily. And so there is a great deal of that kind of process that occurs after death, and then, when you come to the right time, you will be reborn. There is a cycle of coming back into bodies – reincarnation. This is a truth where the soul projects itself once again into manifestation. The soul manifests itself once again into physical reality, whether on the earth, or planet, whatever it is, but it will take on some degree of physicality to evolve.*

ON ENLIGHTENMENT

ORTAN: *Enlightenment is a natural movement of all sentient beings. It is a natural movement to the light. It is the natural movement as the plant unfolds in the sunshine and flowers. This is the same process for you.*

As you unfold in the light you will flower, and that flowering you call on your earth plane 'enlightenment'. The essence of enlightenment is to be completely and utterly clear in all the bodies – complete clarity, grasping and holding on to nothing: not holding on to your personality, not holding on to your opinions, not holding on to your money, or your loved ones, holding nothing, being pure and perfectly centred in heart. Enlightenment will come to all in time. Some have chosen to return as enlightened beings and masters on your earth plane. There are living masters at this time who are enlightened. You can meet them and study with them. You can be with them and, by the resonance of their being, you can start to let go of some of the things that you need to release. You can tune in to the enlightened masters in your meditation, and by reaching to their hearts they will start to teach you.

QUESTIONER: What do we need to do so that we don't have to keep coming back to this earth?

ORTAN: *You need genuinely and sincerely to desire total service to the light, and through service and unselfish giving and working towards your enlightenment, then you will no longer need to return. When you have been through all the lessons, when you have flowered in the light and when you have served humanity, you will no longer need to return. But service is at the heart of that, and, strangely, many of those who do not have to return choose to return again and again as part of their service, beloveds, as part of their service.*

ON PAST LIFE CHANNELLING

ORTAN: *Past life influences on a present life can be very deep and very profound, especially if you have had many lives working on this area. What is important, though, to remember is that all you need to know will be here in the present. If you work with a therapist, the past life issues that are informing the present life will come out. They may not come out as past life issues, but you can heal in the present everything from the past, and indeed you can heal your future too. So just because you are bound in time, it is not something that will hinder your healing or your growth. It was a choice you made to live in a universe of this type, bound within this dimension of time, but it does not stop those past life issues and patterns coming up for healing right now.*

So it is not necessary to spend a lot of money on a past life regression, and past life therapy, and past life everything. If that were necessary, you would have been given the tools yourself by the divine creator. It is not necessary. All that is necessary is the present healing, and into it will come all that needs to be released.

The following channelling was given in response to a question from one of our students about past lives which related to this life and to an activation that was happening to her at that time. It gives an idea of how Ortan works with his clients in this context.

ORTAN: *There are several lifetimes that are relevant. We will enumerate just the points, if you like, the highlights, otherwise we will be here a very long time, will we not? So let us tune in now. Allow yourself to tune in. Good.*

Being within the cocoon of the light body now as we start to move through space and time, we are drawn to a star, a star of such beauty, an exquisite, blazing light in the sky, as we fly through deep space and time, back, back, back through the millenniums to this brilliant star of light. You are a child of this star who chose the activation path all those millions of years ago.

We are inside a temple now. All is white, it is almost dazzling, there is so much light in the temple. In the centre of the temple is a glowing sphere. The sphere is quite clear, it looks like clear quartz, but deep in the heart of this sphere is a glowing light. The light is radiating from this globe, filling the circular room with light. About this circle are many white columns, and when you look up they are lost in the mists of light.

You are standing close to the sphere. You are wearing a white robe. You are deeply moved. The tears are rolling down your cheeks. You are wearing a single pendant. It too is the shape of the globe, a circle of light, and it too is pulsing light activated by your heart chakra. Your hands are raised and you are drawing down the energies, activating the globe. You are a channel of light on a distant star. You are alone in the temple. It is your moment of vow. You are taking a vow of service to the light. You are proving to the universe that you are ready by activating the globe. The small globe you carry upon your chest is the miniature version of the activating globe and the light goes out from that temple, radiating into the solar system. Do you remember the lifetime, dear one?

QUESTIONER: I am very moved.

ORTAN: *It is an old memory, very deep within your DNA. The activation of that light is of great importance at this time, for that light is reaching this planet now, and you are channelling it once more. You are connected into the pure feminine energy through this ray. The ray is very special and the activation is nearly completed.*

It is most important, dear one, that you continue to develop the work of the feminine side. This is your role as a child in this brotherhood. You are a goddess upon the earth plane. You carry within you the heart of the goddess, of all the light of the feminine, and there is more to this light than just that simple manifestation of the goddess, is there not? It is a very complex range of activities now that are needed from you.

Allow yourself to stay within the light body as we assist a final link in with this light. Open your heart. The light is focusing upon you, moving into your light body. The light of that distant star is triggering the codes in your DNA, dear one, a very subtle and profound activation. Take a deep breath now as you breathe this activation through the physical body, letting it run through the spine and through the nerves of the physical body as the activation takes place, moving into the heart of every cell, filling it with the light of the star, and your heart is radiating the light of the star. You are the star in human form. You can feel the star at the heart of every cell, deep in your heart, radiating light now, and feel the final activation of the ajna [third eye or sixth chakra] as you are opening to remember, remembering, opening to a being of light, to the third eye, carrying all the memories you will ever need encoded directly into the cells of your body. Moving in now.

All right. The remembering, dear one, will come when you need it. Do not try to force the process. This is an energy encoding that you have just experienced. Breathe into your heart now, letting it integrate into the body – you may feel a tingling or a lightness. You are quite safe. All right. Shall we play a little more now, dear one?

There is another lifetime that you need to connect with. All right. You are lying in the dark. Find yourself. It is Egypt. You are deep within the heart of the pyramid and you have chosen this process of initiation. You lie in the dark for several days. Your breathing is very slow. Your hands are folded upon your breast and you are holding in your hands the sacred ankh [symbol of life in ancient Egypt]. Upon your forehead is a snake and round your neck is a sacred necklace of lapis.

Your body is very disciplined. It is hard, it is strong. You are very, very, disciplined in this life. Your focus of will is second to nothing. You have great power. You are a servant of the light and you know it. You have chosen this lifetime to hone your ability to the finest possible point. Your speech is strong. You do not speak that much. Every word is chosen by your will.

In the dark you await the activation of your heart and your final initiation into the light. The wait is very long and you do not care. You know that you will die or you will live, and you do not mind for there is no difference in your brave heart. But you understand, dear one, that you do find the light.

Your initiation is successful and you rise to become one who is much respected in that time and within those circles. You are little known beyond the circles of your temple. Your influence is very great, but in a very humble way. You are a person of complete humility, completely dedicated to the service of the light. Your ego does not exist.

In that lifetime in Egypt you lived for a very, very long time – more than a hundred years, dear one. And the initiations that you put others through brought them to the light, although they were hard and you wept much for them. When it came to yourself, you had no mercy. You were like a statue.

All through your life you retained this focus of will, and you chose after that, that all the incarnations upon the earth plane would be in service to the light. You made a vow once more, but this time you were no longer upon the star, you were within the earth plane sphere. So you renewed the vow from the point of view of mankind.

You have had many lifetimes since that dim and distant time in Egypt. You have had lifetimes within many magical traditions. You have had lifetimes across many countries on this planet. You have had a lifetime in Australia, you connect in very much with the energy of that. You have had a lifetime learning the Mayan techniques and processes, and you have had a lifetime with the North American Indians.

Your training, dear one, has been very rigorous, and has reflected the force of your will. For this lifetime you chose a female body, because you felt and understood that it was the feminine energy that was more important, if you like, in the cycle, for it is through the feminine energy that the cycle will be completed.

The rule of men is not so long. Men upon this planet at this time are anchors and balances. It is important that there is male energy, but it is women who will take the planet forward at this time. Hence their importance in all the movements upon the earth at this time.

ON FREQUENCY

ORTAN:　*For the universe as you know it is made up of energy, and the nature of this energy varies across the fabric of the dimensions. Within the dimension that you inhabit the importance of the nature of this energy cannot be over-stressed. This energy vibrates at different rates, at different frequencies, and hence the importance of this term 'frequency' in the teachings that we are giving to you from our dimension. For all the difference between everything that exists within your universe is based on this idea of frequency. And you can see in your daily life how one frequency can give rise, or give birth, to another.*

So let us return to the beginning of this discussion – the nature of the universe. It is such that all that you can see about you vibrates at a different frequency. And you have been equipped with sensory perceptions that enable you to detect these differences in frequency. You are able to see a certain spectrum of frequency, to hear a certain vibratory frequency, to feel the nature of these frequencies through the skin and the touch. And also you have other sense perceptions which are developing, which rely on understanding the inner nature of some of these vibratory subtleties. For they move into another dimension which you are starting to perceive.

And in your universe the planet earth has her own frequency and she vibrates at a particular rate. And hence you could say that this planet has a song within the spheres. And when we talk of the song of the spheres we are talking of the vibration which is given off by discrete planetary units. By discrete things within matter if you like.

Your sun too has a particular energy signature which draws us to it, which draws many creatures, many beings of light and many other beings to it. For this sun signals the presence of you, of you humans, of you intelligences being present. For the sun, if you like, has called you to be present. For without the sun, of course, you could not sustain life on your planet with your present stage of technology. And indeed it is possible to use the solar energy to recharge yourselves, and for us also to draw sufficient energy to make the translation into your dimension. And [so] as we move from our frequencies into yours we draw upon this solar energy. And you will find that solar energy is of great importance in many esoteric disciplines upon the earth plane for this reason. For the frequency of solar energy is the frequency of light and of growth. It is the frequency of assisting others, of service, of love.

Whereas the frequency of the moon is more subtle, if you like – we would say, a different frequency – and those who worship the moon also are those who can assist others, but they do it in their secretive way. So the moon is a more hidden energy, hidden by the sun's rays and the brilliance of the sun. And so it is no accident that these two bodies look so different, for you see you are given these sensory perceptual abilities such as sight to enable you to see that this truly is different. And if you were to listen to them through one of your clever telescopes, you would no doubt be able to find astronomers who would tell you they sound different. And so you are able to look at the planets in a different way now – look at their songs.

And you will see also the importance of frequency of sound on the earth plane. And we have perhaps only hinted to you of the importance of this so far, but you are now starting to discover that this frequency of sound has much to offer in assisting others in their change. You already use the frequency of music, and the channelled music particularly you find beneficial, because the guide who is assisting the human who brings these frequencies to the earth plane is showing him ways to manipulate sound to take people into other states of consciousness or to enable them to perceive other things. There is also the frequency of other types [of things] such as the frequency of thought.

ON PLANES, DIMENSIONS AND WORKING WITH OUR THOUGHTS

ORTAN: There are different planes wherein dwell different levels of being, although it is wrong to assume that everything is ordered *and hierarchical. In terms of planes there is your earth plane, of course, where you dwell within the three dimensions, and there are other planes which resonate at different frequencies. Like, for example, the astral plane, much of that which exists upon the astral plane is created from the earth plane. And this, of course, is one of the reasons that we have said to you that it is important to control the thoughts.*

For negative thoughts and positive thoughts are not differentiated between. And the energy of thought feeds the astral plane and these thoughts can form beings upon that plane, beings, quite empty beings, not motivated by a soul. But they are motivated by the kind of energy that has formed them. And thus if a group were to get together and focus upon negative thoughts they could create some kind of form upon the astral plane. They could open the doorway between the planes and then use the energy of that creation to create difficulties and havoc upon the earth plane. Hence the importance of forming groups to have positive thoughts to assist in positive growth and to counteract the negativity of those who believe that all is doom and destruction. For indeed if you all believe this it will be so. For you create your own reality entirely and part of this creation process is between, is done by the interaction between the astral and the earth plane.

ORTAN: *For the universe is not at all as you think it is, and it is difficult for the human brain to see quite how the universes and dimensions are interwoven. And this interweaving causes anomalies to the human brain in the sense that the future and the past do not exist separately, that you could see and live a past life in the future because of the nature of that dimension that you call time. It is not at all linear. It is very much, as we will call it, woven – intertwined along with other dimensions.*

QUESTIONER: So would people eventually reach where you are through spiritual growth? When you pass over you go the realm of spirit, and do you need to keep reincarnating to reach where you are?

ORTAN: *Indeed. It is very much dependent on the individual soul's state of evolution, for some souls need to be incarnated upon the earth plane for the particular lessons that they need to incorporate in their energy and for the particular experiences that are needed for the evolution of that soul. Other souls, beyond a certain point, will be able to evolve through the dimensions without further rebirth. Other souls again choose to be reborn. They have chosen service to humanity, and they choose to return even though they are enlightened and evolved souls and they could exist in our realms.*

QUESTIONER: When I am meditating and go to the higher realms, and when I see high beings, there's a great high being that comes to see me . . . whatever it is. But they all look the same and so it is difficult to distinguish the difference – fantastic eyes, very tall and a lot of light.

ORTAN: *You see, all of this perception of other beings is very, very limited by your physical reality. When we talk of 'seeing', it is because this is the language of physical reality. We talk of sensing, it is the language of physical reality. We do not 'see' in your sense at all in the way that you do, and when you sense us it is very much bounded by your own brain structure, by your own experiences, and by your own expectations.*

I will tell you a story, dear one, to illustrate this. We have a very dear student who has had many pictures drawn of me, and I have had much amusement with her. And every picture she has had drawn has been very different. She has been to many psychic artists on the earth plane. Each has produced a different picture, and she also has another picture of me in her own mind. And as I have said to her, it doesn't matter, I am all of those and none of those, as all beings are all the things you perceive and none of the things you perceive. . . . I would say to you that the eyes carry so much when you are in physical reality that it is not surprising that your brain chooses to focus on those aspects of ours, because the eyes in your reality carry much energy, do they not, and they carry the energy of the consciousness looking out of the physical vehicle. And so we are often perceived as eyes, or faces, bright lights, lights around those things and little else. You see the size of our energy – our energy is very vast, as is yours. I will remind you, but you forget to perceive it.

ON THE IMPORTANCE OF THOUGHT AND INTEGRITY

ORTAN: *Now thought is a most important topic; there is much written on this topic. But we wish to say to you it is very important for you to understand that thought is form. And in some ways, depending on the nature of the being doing the perceiving, the thoughts are forms. And it is this basic notion that is already known in some of your esoteric disciplines like white magic.*

For thought, love under will is important. For there is the important focus of love as a creative force. And the concept of love under will, of course, is important with this idea of discipline which bridges those two concepts.

Discipline is something that is lacking in some of the seekers who are now upon the earth plane. Not because there is something wrong with them, but because they have not been shown the joyful route of discipline. They see discipline as difficult, as hard. But it is important that they start to understand that when thoughts are random, when they are uncontrolled in the sense that the person thinking them is under the influence of the personality, then they can be dangerous, if you like to put it this way, for they can carry the person away. Thought precedes the action, action then creates the form upon the earth plane. So this movement of thought to action to manifest form is an important progression for people to understand. For example you are hungry, and you think of food, you take action, you go, you find the food and you eat it. And you can be more subtle – you can think of different types of food you would like to eat.

Now the thing is to be careful about what action you take upon the thought. Not that any harm will come to you in a lasting way, but more that it will make things more focused and easier for you to move through, if, when you have thoughts, you always move into a harmonized space connecting it with the higher aspects of yourself, and you recalculate that thought form or pattern if you like and check that it is indeed the one that is most beneficial. And here we come to the issue of integrity.

Integrity is most important, for without integrity, of course, you could create anything you wished, but it may not be of benefit to you and it may not be of benefit to others around you. And so integrity is that manifestation upon the earth plane of the concepts of cooperation, caring, nurturing, loving, taking care of others as if they were your own children. For this is most important – to love others and to support them. And your thoughts, you see, dear ones, are the starting point for this. By maintaining a connection with the higher realms and higher aspects of yourself you can stay in integrity, aligned with higher will and divine energy.

Hence the emphasis we put again and again on moving away from negative thoughts, from thoughts of 'I cannot', 'I cannot do this', 'I should not do this', 'I must not do this'. Or negative thoughts where you think of another, 'He is not as good as me', 'He is not very nice', etc. These are not useful. It is more useful to say, 'He is different', 'I do not understand him', and this will be more useful than saying, 'He is bad', 'He is horrible', 'I do not like him', 'Why does he do this?'. Leave him, let him do what he wishes. It is a free will universe, as we are always saying to you. Releasing yourselves from worrying about others in the sense of judging them or trying to figure them out is helpful.

The discipline of meditation is very important and that these disciplined meditations are carried out every day. It is no good people saying, 'I have not time for this, that and the other'. We are saying to you, 'Come, we call you, it is your time, choose growth. Here is how it may be done. And a simple easy route is meditation.'

ON THE CHAKRAS

QUESTIONER: Now to a question a little more on a human level. I wish I was not so easily put down by others. I feel that it blocks my success in many things that I do. How can I help myself get over this?

ORTAN: *There are two aspects to your question. The first aspect is that everybody upon the earth plane has lessons in growth to learn. This is part of what is happening to you here. You are being offered a lesson, a lesson in trust, a lesson in trusting yourself. This is really what is being offered when these people are putting you down. Learning to trust yourself is a big part of your journey at this time, learning to have confidence in your abilities is part of your growth at this time. We do not mean arrogance, not at all. You can still have great humility, but trust your abilities all the same, trusting your connection to the higher realms and trusting God to take care of you and your needs, to bring the wisdom that you need to answer a question from another.*

The other aspect that is noticeable when we have scanned your energy is that some of the lower chakras need more attention. Specifically the second and third chakras are in need of more balance and alignment. So we would recommend that you spend some time working specifically with chakra energy, and addressing the second and third chakras, even the first as well, for you could be bringing a little more energy through this chakra. There are different routes that you can use to work with the chakras.

You are probably well aware of these routes. I will tell them to you anyway, and you can just ignore it if it is something you know. We strongly recommend the use of Reiki with the chakras. Using Reiki into the chakras is very simple, very strengthening and a direct link to source energy. We also recommend the use of crystals. The way that crystals can channel the energy through the chakra is very powerful and yet subtle. The vibration of the crystals is particularly good for this, as you know. The third way is meditation, and we strongly recommend meditation with the energy of the chakras [which] will be helpful for you to assist in building your confidence.

ON THE SOUL AND THE HIGHER SELF

QUESTIONER: Does the higher self use the intuition to get through to you.

ORTAN: *Indeed, for the soul, the higher self and guides, the only route through to the mind is through what the psychologists on the earth plane call the right brain. It is through those subtle nudges, those sudden insights and those feelings that you cannot substantiate but you know are right. These are the subtle intonations of the other side, of the higher self, the soul and the guide.*

The connection with the higher self has to be made consciously by the individual, and so that connection you could describe as being like a channel of light that is sent upwards from the crown chakra to the higher self, and it has been called by mystics in your earth plane the antakarana. The antakarana, dear one, is the cord of light between your physical body and the energy of your soul. The building of the antakarana is a key process in esoteric tradition, for good reason, because it is through this cord of light that you connect fully with the soul and are able to draw yourself fully into union with it. There is a question of the soul moving down and you moving up, for you must remember that the soul is not interested in you at all. You are interested in your soul but your soul is quite happy; you must draw the soul in.

On Guides' View of Humans

QUESTIONER: Do you actually see us as humans in human form, or do you see us as light?

ORTAN: *We see you as energy. And you could describe it as eggs. We see you as egg-shaped energy beings.*

On the Soul Path

QUESTIONER: Is there such a thing as being on the wrong soul path? We seem to have a lot of choices given to us in life, and sometimes we look back and wonder whether we should have gone along a certain path. Could it be that we are on the wrong path? Or should we be on that path to learn those lessons?

ORTAN: *There is no such thing as the wrong path, for all choices are made at the time, with the energy of that time, with the knowledge of that time. And many humans suffer from regret and guilt and sadness, but what is the point of these emotions? For we are in the present, in the here and now, and looking back into the past is not a useful practice. Although the lessons will be learnt in the time of the present they will not be learnt in the past, for they are, if you like, a movement of energy as you move through it. You are in it, you have the experience, and you move to the next experience. Life is lived moment to moment in the present.*

Dear one, there can be no wrong path and no wrong decisions. All is done in perfection for your soul, and your energy will bring you to have those experiences that will most assist your growth. Your person-ality may cry out, 'I do not wish to have this experience', but the soul will inexorably guide it to have the next lesson. If you refuse to learn the lesson, if your personality will not integrate the lesson, then you will be given the lesson again and again, maybe through many lifetimes until finally you accept it with gratitude and with love. And, dear one, know that the secret of all spiritual growth is to be grateful to God for all that you are given, whatever it is, and to open your heart in love to all sentient beings.

ON PAST LIFETIMES

QUESTIONER: When we talk other lifetimes, often we talk about past lifetimes. Other sources talk about parallel lifetimes. Are we present in other dimensions simultaneously?

ORTAN: *Of course. Where do you think you are? Do you think you are a physical body? Your question is, 'How many lifetimes am I having at once?' and 'Where am I?'*

QUESTIONER: Yes: where am I? And if I'm changing in one area, how does that affect the other areas?

ORTAN: *Yes, yes, yes. Good question. This question of time is a little bit tricky, is it not? You see, when you were born into this lifetime, you chose to be on a time line. You said, 'I know, I know, I know it's going to be hard, but I will go for it.' When you were a soul, of course, you had no idea what this was going to involve. When you came back you suddenly went, 'Oh, yes, I am in the time line.'*

This time line is part of the nature of your physicality. As a physical being you cannot be sitting here in this room and having a conversation with me and be in Australia. Not possible – unless you cut yourself up, of course. But your consciousness can't do that in the physical body; it has to release itself from the physical body.

You, of course, can be in many places at once even from the physical body, as you train yourself. Consciousness has no boundaries, no limits and no places it has to be. It is only the physical stuff that has the tricky problem here. Do you get this [questioner nods assent]? Ah. Good.

So, consciousness can be in many, many places, and is in many, many places. Your consciousness has a little bit of an awareness of this room, a little bit of awareness of itself, and of yourself as a multi-dimensional being of light. That is what you are, and you exist through many planes, many planes and places of reality, and so you are going on at once in many, many places.

The physical body is just a boundary that you have chosen to work with. You came here to have the lessons that physicality brings to you. One of those lessons is what it is to be constrained within a dimension, the dimension of time. When people talk of parallel lives it is perfectly valid, it is perfectly reasonable to see that, because from our perspective time is not in a line, not linear, and we could say the past is the future, the present is the past.

This is very confusing and not useful for the brain to think of, is it? I suggest to you that you think of yourself as a dispersed, multi-dimensional matrix of consciousness being, and that your physical body is stuck in the time line. The rest of you, fortunately, is not. So these lives are existing all at once, but they aren't because there's only one body.

ON ANIMALS

QUESTIONER: Do animals get the opportunity to incarnate as humans?

ORTAN: *Interesting question. No. Do you wish me to elaborate? You see, the animals are sentient beings like you. They didn't want to be humans. There are many, many interesting beingnesses within the animal kingdom, and they like to be animals and they have chosen service. Many of them have chosen a deep level of service. As you observe how much they suffer on your earth plane, how much they serve you, and what great companions they are to you and to your kind.*

But the animals are part of another realm of beingness, and they don't wish to be involved with the human experience in terms of being it, but they are with you, just as the plants are with you and the crystals are with you and the earth is with you. They are different realms, different kingdoms, and their frequency is that of the angelic realms, and so when they pass from having a physical life, many of them move into being angelics. They have those kinds of frequencies of the angelic realms, just as the plants are angelic, just as the crystals are

*angelic, so too the animals are angelic, so the different realm of
beingness, are not better, not worse, just different than those souls who
have incarnated through the human route.*

ON THE SOUL

QUESTIONER: Is there such a thing as an individual soul, or are
we all aspects of one soul?

ORTAN: *That is a good question. There is an All That Is source, the
basic source from which all has emanated. Every one of you and
myself are part of that source. You could see us like sparks flying from
the fire, and the fire is the source. Each spark has an individual,
apparently individual reality, but it will always eventually come
back. As it lands and it ignites, the whole thing becomes the source.
Do you see what I am saying?*

  *You therefore have an individual reality, you have an individual
beingness, and you have a total connection with All That Is, for all of
us are just one consciousness, or one beingness, if you like, a beingness
that has chosen to experience in many different and myriad ways. But
all will be drawn back in to that All That Is source eventually, until
once again it breathes out and more manifestation will take place. At
the present time you are on the in breath, and all are journeying
home. That is why it is called the journey home. It is the journey back
to source.*

ON REINCARNATION

QUESTIONER: Do we have one individual reality from one
incarnation to the next?

ORTAN: *Each incarnation feels individual, does it not? That is the
nature of it. It is the casting away from source. The further away you
get, the more individual you feel, but that is only an illusion. That is
again to return to this question here. It is the question of enlightenment – being within this world, being alone, isolated. This is an illusion. There is no such thing as this isolation. Through your channelling
you are starting to sense that, are you not? You are not alone at all. In*

our dimension we are all here and we are here now, but you just don't see us or notice us. But you're not alone, and your beingness is not alone. You are not separate, you are part of the oneness.

QUESTIONER: So with every rebirth there is an individual reality or spark.

ORTAN: *Yes. Well, you know that, you're in one. You feel it. You see, you are so immersed in the illusion you think that's all there is, don't you? You're forgetting, forgetting, forgetting what you are. This makes it hard for you, for some of the lessons, you see, are about understanding that, and realizing the illusion of that.*

ON SOUL GROUPS AND SOUL MATES

QUESTIONER: People often speak about soul groups, and at this time there is much written about soul mates and twin souls and suchlike. What are your comments on it?

ORTAN: *Soul groups are groups of souls who, when not upon the earth plane, have perhaps been doing some work together, who have chosen to do some work together, and who are incarnating together. Perhaps through many lifetimes these soul groups, loosely associated together, will come and be born together, then will meet again and will like each other. They will be friends, they will be colleagues, they will be married to each other, they will have children together and so on. These soul groups continuously are reborn together, and if you start to look at your past lives, you will start to notice. You'll think, 'Aha, there is so-and-so.' You will recognize them. They may not look the same, but you will know their energy.*

So there are definitely soul groups, groups of souls who are in alignment. You see, you could say that groups of souls have an interest. Some groups of souls have an interest in science. Some groups of souls have an interest in nature, and in crystals, and in healing. You know there are many, many groups, without going into long details about these groups, and masters teach these groups when they're not upon the earth plane and when they are sleeping and so on, when the conscious mind is out of the way. And so these soul groups are continuously manifesting.

Soul mates, on the other hand, is a different topic – many who come to readings ask me about their soul mates. 'Have I got a soul mate? Where is my soul mate? Why can't I have a soul mate?' is a very popular topic: 'I want more of them.' And we observe this and we understand that the desire for union, the desire for the journey home, is what they are really talking about. They are really missing the one-ness, and it manifests on your earth plane as a desire for a soul mate, but it is best to go for a partner. You know, the soul mate concept is very alluring, but it is appealing to a deeper need within you. That need is the need for spiritual growth.

On Disease and Suffering

QUESTIONER: There is much disease on the planet at this moment. With all the new energies that are coming in, will we see a clearance of a lot of these diseases that we now have?

ORTAN: *Many diseases are caused, of course, by decay within the genetic structure of the body, and it is natural, and part of the process of letting go of the physical, to learn that things are born and they decay, and they become diseased and die. And of course as you have become more advanced in your ability to heal, people live longer and have even more diseases because they have the diseases of a longer-lived body, and this is simply the way that it is for physicality. It is not perfect, it is not held in perfection, because it is all subject to change, to corruption, to decay. And it is natural, this cycle of physicality, it is a physical cycle.*

However, as things are changing, and as I mentioned a little while ago when I was saying to you that the earth is ascending and your planet is ascending and that your people are ascending, there will be physical changes, and these are the type of physical changes I was referring to. Because part of the physical changes will come from your advances in your ability to understand the genetic cycle. And there are great advances taking place and about to take place in your understanding of the genetic cycles and how they work, and this great ability to change the genetic structure of your race is going to be tremendously beneficial. Do not pooh-pooh your science. Many of your scientists are wonderful channels and are bringing through so much information now for use upon the earth plane to alleviate the suffering of genetic disease. Much disease is based within genetics.

Some disease, of course, dear one, is caused by abuse of the physical body. People are abusing their bodies and making themselves sick and that is their choice, so we can't take that away from them. They are taking drugs, they are taking alcohol, they are smoking, they are not exercising, all of the things that you know about. In the ascension process, therefore, people will become less ill, because they will not choose to abuse themselves, and because of these genetic changes that we have mentioned. And because there will be so much more understanding in the next hundred years, your sciences will undergo tremendous changes, and so the answer is yes, there will be less of it. . . .

We are finishing now, dear ones. Let us just bring our awareness back into the heart. I thank each of you for your beautiful questions, for it is a great joy to me to share energy with you, each of you being a beautiful and perfect channel of light. Spend a moment to tune into your perfection, for from our perspective each of you is pure beauty, each of you is a perfect soul, and we observe your struggle with physicality and our heart is with you in that struggle. For we see how difficult it is for you to be away from home, to be there in that body, and we hold you in our heart.

GLOSSARY

Antakarana   The cord of light between the physical body and the energy of the soul.

Arhat (Lord of Compassion)   The title applied to a person who has reached the fourth initiation.

Ascended Masters   Those who have become one with the divine light as a result of their work on themselves through many lifetimes. They have ascended into the presence of God, but continue to teach.

Ascension   The process whereby we lift our own vibration through spiritual work and growth until we reach the presence of God. The process involves holding more and more light through all the bodies – physical, emotional, mental and spiritual.

Astral Plane   The point reached when a person has gained mastery over their emotions and desires.

Atlantis   An ancient civilization that flourished for many years, using advanced technologies involving crystalline energy. They failed to balance their growth with spiritual practices and so were doomed to sink beneath the ocean. Some did escape the terrible cataclysm that engulfed Atlantis and fled to Egypt, Greece and America.

Aura/Auric Field The energy field which surrounds your physical body.

Bodhisattvas These are people who will become buddhas, but to do so they have to work with the qualities of morality, charity, wisdom, unconditional love, patience, truth, renunciation, will and composure.

> *The Bodhisattva Vow*
> With the wish to free all beings
> I shall always go for Refuge
> To the Buddha, Dharma and Sangha
> Until the attainment of full enlightenment
>
> Enthused by compassion and wisdom
> Today in the Buddha's presence
> I generate the Mind of Enlightenment
> For the benefit of all sentient beings
>
> As long as space endures
> And as long as sentient beings remain
> May I, too, abide
> To dispel the miseries of the world.

Caduceus The wand of the healer.

Chakra A centre of force located throughout the auric layers/bodies.

Channel A person with the ability to hold and maintain a conscious connection with a guide from the higher realms.

Earth Plane The plane in which humans exist.

Guide   A being who has chosen to work with humans to enable them to access high-level information to assist their growth.

Higher Self   An aspect of a person's energy that is at a lower dimensional level than the soul and close to the physical self.

Kabbalah   An ancient Jewish system based on the Tree of Life.

Karma   The balance of spiritual credits and debits accumulated in a lifetime created by a person's thoughts and actions.

Kundalini   The awakening of the energy which lies within the base chakra.

Light Body   A form of spiritual body which reflects the true nature of the soul. This body allows interdimensional travel and communication with entities from other dimensions.

Monad   Soul's soul.

New Age   The current time in which the frequencies bombarding the planet are shifting and changing leading to a greater awareness of the spiritual dimension of life.

Nirvana   A Buddhist concept: a state of blissful consciousness achieved through meditation.

NLP (Neuro Linguistic Programming)   A branch of psychology/personal growth movement founded by Richard Bandler and John Grinder.

Planetary Logos   A Planetary Logos is like the soul of a planet. As we are souls in physical bodies, so the Planetary Logoi are also souls with the planet as their physical body. The Planetary Logos for the earth is Sanat Kumara.

Prana/Pranayama   Life force energy which can be directed and controlled by breathing exercises.

Reiki   A form of healing where the practitioner channels the Reiki energy through the hands to assist the client's healing process.

Sarasvati   The 'channel of fire' which runs straight up the centre of the physical body from the first to the seventh chakra and connects them all.

Solar Logos   The Solar Logos is Helios. The Solar Logos is a Master with the cosmic responsibility for the frequencies associated with our sun (see Planetary Logos).

Sushumna   A subtle channel in the body.

Theosophy   A system founded in the nineteenth century by Madame Blavatsky, based on Indian religious philosophy. It holds that we can achieve wisdom, and an understanding of the nature of God, through yoga.

Third Eye   A chakra in the centre of the forehead. It is also known as the ajna centre, and it is where your psychic abilities can be awakened.

Universal Mind   Also known as the Karmic Records, this is the dimension where all that has been known and that will be known is available.

Vibrational Frequency   The rate at which the atoms and particles vibrate. The higher the frequency, the nearer to the light one is. Hence guides vibrate at much higher rates than human beings.

White Magic   A Western approach to spiritual growth based on the Kabbalah, meditation and service to the light.

BIBLIOGRAPHY

ANODEA, Judith. *Wheels of Life: A User's Guide to the Chakra System.* St. Paul: Llewellyn, 1993.

BAILEY, Alice. *Initiation: Human and Solar.* New York: Lucis Publishing Company, 1977.

———. *The Light of the Soul.* New York: Lucis Publishing Company, 1989.

BRENNAN, Barbara. *Hands of Light.* New York: Bantam, 1998.

BUTLER, W. E. *Lords of Light: The Path of Initiation in the Western Mysteries.* Rochester, VT: Destiny Books, 1990.

GOLDSTEIN, Joseph. *Insight Meditation: The Practice of Freedom.* Dublin, Ireland: Gill & Macmillan, 1993.

HANH, Thich Nhat. *The Blooming of a Lotus: Guided Meditation Exercises for Healing and Transformation.* Boston: Beacon Press, 1993.

———. *Transformation and Healing: Sutra on the Four Establishments of Mindfulness.* Albany, CA: Parallax Press, 1990.

OZANIEC, Naoma. *The Elements of the Chakras.* Boston: Element, 1990.

KORNFIELD, Jack. *A Path with Heart: The Perils and Promises of Spiritual Life*. New York: Bantam, 1993, London: Rider, 1994.

REGARDIE, Israel. *The Art and Meaning of Magic*. Cheltenham, Glos., England: Helios, 1964.

———. *Foundations of Practical Magic*. London: Aquarian Press, 1982.

ROMAN, Sanaya. *Living With Joy: Keys to Personal Power and Spiritual Transformation*. Tiburon, CA: H. J. Kramer, 1986.

ROMAN, Sanaya and Duane Parker. *Opening to Channel: How to Connect with Your Guide*. Tiburon, CA: H. J. Kramer, 1987.

STONE, Joshua. *The Complete Ascension Manual: How to Achieve Ascension in This Lifetime*. Sedona, AZ: Light Technology Publishing, 1994.

THESENGA, Susan. *The Undefended Self: Living the Path of Spiritual Wholeness*. Del Mar, CA: Pathwork Press, 1994.

WHITE, Ruth. *Working with Your Chakras: A Physical, Emotional and Spiritual Approach*. York Beach, ME: Samuel Weiser, 1994.

INDEX

THE SCHOOL OF
THE LIVING LIGHT

To receive a free newsletter and for more information about courses and tapes, please contact:

Lita de Alberdi
The School of the Living Light
47 Aldreth Road
Haddenham
Cambridgeshire CB6 3PW
United Kingdom

Telephone: 011-44-1353-741760
Fax: 011-44-1353-741782
www.living-light,com

The School of the Living Light, founded in 1994, has a comprehensive mail order catalogue of courses on tape, meditation tapes by Lita and by Sanaya Roman and Duane Packer, channels for Orin and DaBen respectively, relaxation tapes, books, channelled music, and lots more. Write or call for a catalogue.

Lita de Alberdi is a gifted Light Body teacher who spends her time channelling, teaching, healing, and doing spiritual counseling at the School of the Living Light, which she founded in 1994. Her unique approach to energy work is the result of more than 25 years of study in psychology, sociology, yoga, meditation, healing, Eastern mysticism, and Western esoteric traditions. She lives in London.

Achevé d'imprimer au Québec
en mai 2013 sur papier Enviro Édition
par l'imprimerie Gauvin.